Trivial Pursuit™ Trivial Pursuit™ Trivial

Trivial Pursuit™ Trivial Pursuit™ Trivial Pursuit™

Pursuit™ Trivial Pursuit™ Trivial Pursuit™ Trivial

Trivial Pursuit™ Trivial Pursuit™ Trivial Pursuit™

Pursuit™ Trivial Pursuit™ Trivial Pursuit™ Trivial

Trivial Pursuit™ Trivial Pursuit™ Trivial Pursuit™

Trivial Pursuit ™

YOUNG PLAYERS QUIZ BOOK

YOUNG PLAYERS QUIZ BOOK

GUINNESS BOOKS

Design concept and layout by Craig Dodd

© Guinness Superlatives Ltd and Horn Abbot International Limited 1987
Published in Great Britain by Guinness Superlatives Ltd,
33 London Road, Enfield, Middlesex

Typeset by Keyspools Limited, U.K.
Printed by New Interlitho S.P.A., Italy

British Library Cataloguing in Publication Data
Trivial pursuit: young players quiz book
   1. Children's questions and answers.
   I. Title
   793.73   AG195
   ISBN 0–85112–862–9

Trivial Pursuit is a game and trademark owned and licensed by Horn
Abbot International Limited

HORN ABBOT
INTERNATIONAL

Contents

At last it's here, the book that all young quiz fans have been waiting for: **Trivial Pursuit — The Young Players Quiz Book**, brought to you by Guinness , the Publishers of the world's best-selling book — *The Guinness Book of Records*. Now quiz whizz kids from the age of eight and upwards have their own Trivial Pursuit edition to carry with them and test their trivia knowledge wherever they go.

This **Young Players Quiz Book** contains 1400 great trivia questions on subjects as varied as television, myths and legends, pop music, simple science, characters from history, space exploration, travel .. 56 truly fiendish quizzes in all, each colourfully illustrated and with detailed answers listed at the back, making it educational and informative as well as fun!

You can use this book as a personal trivia test — see how many questions you can answer in a row or keep a record for your highest score in each quiz — or challenge your friends. Each choose a different quiz and ask the other questions to see who gets most answers right.

However you choose to use this book, you'll find that the quizzes are divided into six Trivial Pursuit categories coded:

PP   People and Places
GT   Good Times
ST   Science and Technology
AC   Art and Culture
NW   Natural World
GH   Games and Hobbies

It's tricky! It's trivial! It's informative! It's fun!

And while you're puzzling over the questions, why not try the Great Cover Quiz? There are 56 quizzes in this book and 56 items or people or animals or places illustrated on the cover. Each illustration corresponds to a particular question or answer in each one of the quizzes. Be careful – we've played a few tricks with some of the pictures just to make it more difficult! Can *you* find them all?

Answers available after 1 February 1988 by writing to this address and enclosing a stamped addressed envelope:

Guinness Books
Cover Quiz Answers
33 London Road
Enfield
Middlesex EN2 6DJ

1. Which New York landmark has a nose 4.5 feet long?

2. Blackfriars, Albert and Hungerford Bridges all span which river?

3. Where would you see this castle overlooking these gardens?
▼

4. In which country are the people known as Monégasques?

5. Which capital city is built on the Seine?

6. Which capital burned while Nero fiddled?

7. Where does this statue stare out to sea? ▶ ▶ ▶

8. Which two countries does the St Bernard Pass connect?

9. Which capital city is also known as Beijing?

10. We call them the Falkland Islands: who calls them the *Islas Malvinas*?

11. Which sea washes the shores of Bulgaria?

12. Where are the antipodes?

13. Haiti and the Dominican Republic are both parts of the same island – which one?

14. If you were surfing on Bondi Beach, where would you be?

15. In which country do people speak Hebrew?

16. If you were in the Granite City, where would you be?
a) Edinburgh   b) Glasgow   c) Aberdeen

17. Where would you most likely be if you were offered *paella* in a restaurant?

18. In which city can you see St Mark's Cathedral and the Doge's Palace?

(23) If you were in the Doldrums, would you be on land, sea or air?

✓ (24) In which country can you kiss the Blarney Stone?

(25) In which modern country is Noah's Ark thought to have reached dry land?
▼

▲

(19) In which city would you be if you were looking at this painting?

(20) There's a statue of Romeo and Juliet in which Italian city?

(21) Where would you be if you were watching someone doing this? ►

(22) Where do Blake and Krystle Carrington, Alexis Colby and Dex Dexter live?

1 Which band has a lead singer called Ben Volpeliere-Pierrot?
▼

2 Which boys had a hit with 'West End Girls'?

3 What are the US record industry's awards called?
a) Grammies   b) Presleys   c) Discoes

4 Who is Police's lead singer?
▼

▲
5 Where did this rock star fall to in one of his movies?

6 Which band walked like an Egyptian?

7 With whom did Stevie Wonder share his first British number one, 'Ebony and Ivory'?
a) Michael Jackson   b) Boy George   c) Paul McCartney

8 Which band went to number one with 'Don't Leave Me This Way'?

9 Who had a hit with his LP *Graceland*?

10 Which of these songs has not been released as a single by Sting?
a) 'Russians'   b) 'Blue Turtle Blues'   c) 'Love is the Seventh Wave'

11 Which group made an album called *Mange Toute*?

12 What were the christian names of the Beatles?
▼

15 Who has had hits with 'White Wedding' and 'To Be a Lover'?

16 Who recorded the hit LP *Can't Slow Down*?

17 Which band's music was featured in the film *The Wall*?

18 Who had a 1984 hit with 'Wild Boys'?

19 Which song, recorded and filmed for the Live Aid concert by David Bowie and Mick Jagger, gave them a number one hit?

20 Which pop group was led by Tony Hadley 'To cut a Long Story Short'?

13 Which group has Phil Collins as lead singer?

14 What was this rock and roll star's nickname?

21 Which Beatles' song was recorded to raise money for victims of the Zeebrugge ferry disaster?

22 Pete Townshend and Roger Daltrey played with which famous band?

23 Who was the great pretender in 1987?

24 Which singer leads the Banshees?

25 How are chart-toppers Doris, Deneice, Lorraine, Steadman and Delroy Pearson better known?

1 What is the biggest muscle in the body?

5 Which of our fingernails grows the fastest?

6 What is the body's normal temperature?

7 What has two auricles and two ventricles?

8 What is it impossible to keep open while sneezing?

9 How did Robert Pershing Wadlow make medical history?

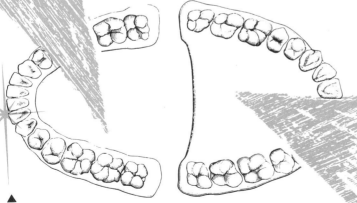

2 How many teeth should we have?

3 Is the liver a muscle or a gland?

4 What is the only muscle that is attached at one end only?

(10) What is the commonest disease in the world?

(11) How many pores do we have?
a) 1 000 000   b) 2 000 000   c) 2 500 000

(12) Who has the heavier brain, a man or a woman?

(13) What was the first vitamin to be discovered?
a) A   b) B   c) B_1

(14) If you suffer from hay fever what are you sensitive to?

(15) What gas do we breathe out?

(16) Water accounts for how much of our body weight?
a) $\frac{1}{2}$ b) $\frac{2}{3}$ c) $\frac{3}{4}$

(17) How many bones are there in the human body?
a) 154   b) 206   c) 254
▼

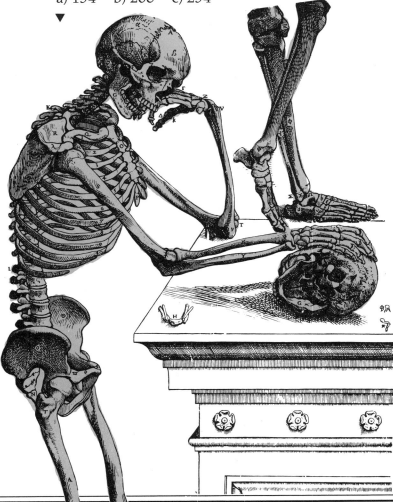

(18) Where would you find the smallest bone in the body?

(19) What does IQ stand for?

(20) What does a surgeon remove during an appendectomy?
▼

(21) Where would you find the sclera, cornea and retina?

(22) What is made of plasma, red corpuscles and white corpuscles?

(23) Which sense develops first?
a) sight   b) touch   c) smell

(24) What are O, A, B and AB?

(25) How much blood do we have?
a) 2.5 litres   b) 4.5 litres   c) 6.5 litres.

√ 1. Where would you wear an epaulette?

2. Who, apart from dogs, wear dog collars?

3. What do we call sailors' trousers?

√ 4. What Central American state gave its name to a straw hat?

5. In Victorian times, would a bustle have been worn by a man or a woman?

6. Is a dirndl?
a) a skirt   b) a waistcoat   c) a jacket

√ 7. What is a trilby?

8. Wellington boots were named after
a) Arthur Wellesley, first Duke of Wellington
b) Horatio Nelson, first Duke of Wellington
c) John Churchill, first Duke of Wellington?
▼

A WELLINGTON BOOT
or the Head of the Armye

9. Who invented the mackintosh?

10. What kind of hat did Sherlock Holmes wear?
a) a deerstalker   b) a sombrero   c) a beret
▼

11. What are Austrian Lederhosen made of?

12. Which clothing company uses this animal as its symbol?
a) Adidas   b) Nike   c) Lacoste
▼

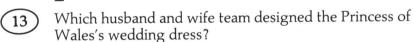
▲

▲

(20) What do we call the face veil worn by Muslim women?

(21) Which type of trousers take their name from an island off the coast of America?

(22) Denim is called denim because
a) it was first produced by Jacques Denim
b) it was first made in the French town of Nîmes
c) It was first made by *David Edward Neil Ian Mason*?

(23) Where would a Scotsman keep his skean-dhu?

(24) Who would you expect to see wearing maternity clothes?

(25) What form of dress do you associate with India?

(13) Which husband and wife team designed the Princess of Wales's wedding dress?

(14) Who would you most likely see wearing a tutu?

(15) What do we call the silk jacket worn by flat-racing ▶ jockeys?

(16) What are clogs made of?

(17) The soldiers of which European country wear white skirts?

(18) What is a corsage?

(19) What kind of heels take their name from a small dagger?

(1) How many chickens are there in the world?
a) 4 500 000   b) 45 000 000   c) 4 500 000 000.

(2) Who wrote *Animal Farm*?

(3) Which farm animals live in a sty?

(4) What are Guernsey, Jersey and Friesian types of?

(5) In what sort of farms are trout and other fish reared?

(6) Which dogs make the best sheepdogs?
▼

(7) What is a male goat called?

(8) Which animals are affected by swine fever?

(9) If a field is lying fallow, what does it lack?

(10) What food crop grows in paddy fields?
▼

(11) Which birds live in a dovecot?

(12) There was a famous eighteenth-century farmer nicknamed after a vegetable. Was he
a) Turnip Townshend   b) Carrot Carter   c) Potato Ponsonby?

▲

13 What colour is a Granny Smith apple?

14 Which farm animals chew the cud?

15 Which of these is a cereal crop?
a) barley   b) cabbages   c) cotton.

16 What do organic farmers avoid using?

17 What are barnyard fowl?

18 What does a farmer keep in a silo?

19 Which government minister is responsible for agriculture?

20 Who looks after goats?

21 What farm did Rebecca live on?

▼

22 What animals would you find in a byre?

23 Rhode Island Reds and Buff Orpingtons are types of what?

24 Which king was known as 'Farmer' George?
a) George I   b) George II   c) George III?

▼

25 What's an arable farm?

1. Which sport is played at Landsdowne Park and Murrayfield?

2. How many balls are on the table during a game of billiards?

3. How many pins are there in ten-pin bowling?

4. Which of the following is not a first-class cricket county?
   a) Somerset   b) Berkshire   c) Kent

5. What's the most important court at Wimbledon? ▼

6. There are twelve players in a women's lacrosse team: how many are there in a men's team?

7. Which soccer team has a cannon on its coat of arms?

8. What colour of ball do you pot to score six in snooker?

9. Tennis stars Ivan Lendl, Martina Navratilova and Hana Mandlikova were all born in which country?

10. How many holes are normally played during a game of golf?

11. How many times are you allowed to bounce the ball in netball before getting rid of it?

12. What game did Tom Cruise play in *The Color of Money*? ▼

(13) If you mishit a snooker ball do you lose points or are they added to your opponent's score?

(14) What colour can 'official' tennis balls be, other than white?

(15) Has a Welsh soccer team ever won the FA cup?

(16) Which American City is the home of baseball teams The Yankees and The Giants?

(17) What does MCC stand for?

(18) Which game is played over the Old and New Courses in St Andrews?

(19) What do badminton players use in place of a ball?

(20) Is there any difference between American Football and Canadian Football?

(21) Which game is played on flat or crown greens?

(22) How many senior titles are played for at Wimbledon every year?

(23) What are the playing periods in a game of polo called? ▶
a) pukkas   b) chukkas   c) rukkas

(24) How many ball games are official Olympic sports?

(25) In which country is hurling a major sport? ▶ ▶

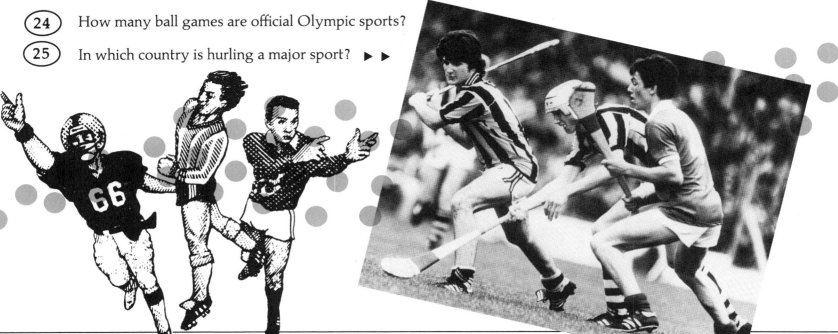

(1) Who is the Bishop of Rome?

(2) Who asked for John the Baptist's head after she danced for her step-father?

(3) What's her first name? Her husband is President of the United States.
▼

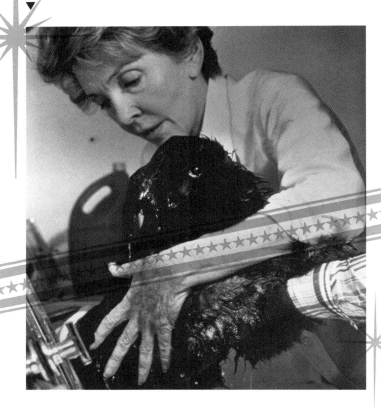

(4) Which French queen is reputed to have said 'Let them eat cake?'

(5) Who was prime minister of Britain for most of World War II?

(6) Her middle name is Hilda. Her husband is called Dennis. Her children are called Mark and Carol. Who is she?

(7) What's his real name?
▼

(8) Who betrayed Jesus to the Romans?

(9) Who became famous for nursing soldiers during the Crimean War?

(10) Who said 'Veni. Vidi. Vici.'

(11) Who was the Queen's first grandchild?

(12) Who was the first man to fly the English Channel?

(13) Whose middle name was Amadeus?

▲

(14) Her first name was Alexandrina and she was Britain's longest reigning monarch. What is her better known name?

(15) Who designed St Paul's Cathedral?

(16) She was Queen of France, Queen of Scotland and wanted to be Queen of England. Who was she?

▼

(17) Who has a newsround on BBC?

(18) Barbara Cartland, the romantic novelist, is related to which English princess?

(19) Who was the first president of the United States?

(20) This Queen of England never married. Who was she?

▼

(21) The Bard of Avon is better known as whom?

(22) Who was the youngest-ever president of the United States?

(23) Who was the first man to walk on the moon?

(24) Who led the 'Desert Rats' against Rommel's Afrika Corps during World War II?

(25) What was the Duchess of York's name before she married Prince Andrew?

▼

① Which group do Morten, Päl and Mags form and where do they come from?

② Which two singers were known as Wham!?

▼

▲

⑥ How many are there in Spandau Ballet?

⑦ Which group takes its name from a Social Security form?

⑧ Cliff Richard and Sarah Brightman, and Michael Crawford have had chart successes with songs from which smash-hit show?

③ Which actor did Michael of Madness sing about?

④ Who No Parlez in 1983? ▶ ▶ ▶ ▶ ▶ ▶

⑤ With which band does Jimmy Somerville sing?

(9) Who is this Material Girl?

▼

(10) What is Bruce Springsteen's band called?

(11) She became famous with her husband Ike before becoming a super-star on her own. Who is she? ►

(12) Peter Gabriel used to be with which group?

(13) What does Michael Jackson turn into in the video *Thriller*?

(14) Daryl and John are the first names of which famous duo?

(15) Where does Frankie go to?

(16) What's odd about the Thompson Twins?

(17) Which two EastEnders have been in the charts?

(18) Alison Moyet used to belong to which group?

(19) Which pop star was knighted?

(20) Which pop star became famous by taking his clothes off in a launderette?

(21) Which band has a lead singer called Bono Vox?

(22) What is the best-selling British single of all time?

(23) Why were Abba so called?

(24) Who is Annie Lennox's partner in the Eurythmics?

(25) What sort of boys are Neil Tennant and Chris Lowe?

√ (1) Is a square always rectangular?

(2) An equilateral triangle has
a) two equal sides   b) no equal sides   c) three equal sides?
▼

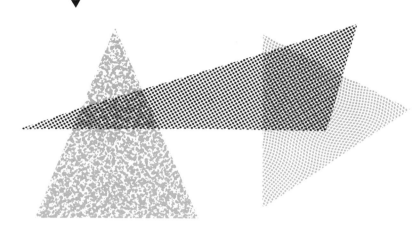

√ (3) How many degrees are there in a circle?

(4) How many sides does a hexagon have?

(5) Does this picture show a cone, a cylinder or a sphere?
▼

(6) What branch of mathematics is concerned with points, lines, curves and surfaces?

(7) If two angles of a triangle add up to 120°, what must the third angle be?

(8) Why is the headquarters of the US armed forces called the Pentagon?
▼

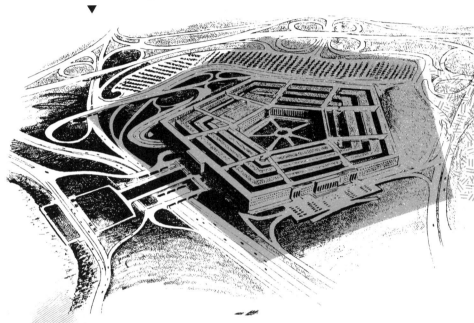

(9) Which is bigger, a cubic metre or a cubic foot?

(10) How many legs does a tripod have?

(11) How many faces does a cube have?
▼

✓ (12) What cricket ground has the shape of an elipse?

(13) What ring has four equal sides of 20 feet each?

(14) What shape were the heads of Cromwell's supporters?
▼

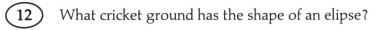

(15) How many sides does an Octogan have?

(16) London's Berkeley, Grosvenor and Belgrave are what?

(17) What shape do we fill with ice-cream?
▼

(18) The Supreme Headquarters for Allied Power Europe is shortened to what?

✓ (19) In what shape of tomb were Egyptian pharaohs buried?

(20) What shape is a satisfying, well-balanced meal?

✓ (21) Where would you find a square leg?

(22) What is the shortest distance between two points?

▲

(23) Where do BBC's EastEnders live?

(24) What famous chocolate bar is triangular in shape?

(25) What disaster-prone area did Barry Manilow have a hit with?

(1) At what age does a Jewish boy have his *Bar Mitzvah*?

(2) What celebration do Americans hold on the fourth Thursday of November?

(3) On what day are Hot Cross Buns traditionally eaten?

(4) What religion is based on the teachings of Confucius?
▼

▲
(7) What major event occurs in Moscow on May Day?

(8) To the followers of which religion is Mecca the Holy City?
▼

(5) In which religion are the *ayatollahs* holy men?
a) Islam   b) Hinduism   c) Judaism

(6) How many disciples did Jesus have?

9 The five whats are important to Sikhs?

10 On which evening do children play Trick or Treat?

11 On what day of the week does the Jewish sabbath fall?

12 What meat do we traditionally serve at Easter?

13 Who introduced the Christmas tree into Britain?

21 Why do we wear wedding rings on the third finger of the left hand?

22 What sort of wreaths do we hang on our doors at Christmas time?

23 How many birthdays does the Queen have each year?

24 What did the winners of Olympic events in Ancient Greece receive?

25 Who is the Defender of the Faith?

14 What large animal's head does the Hindu god of wisdom have?

15 What religion are the Jesuits?

16 After midnight on Hogmanay, Scots call on each others' houses: is this called
a) docking the doris   b) Caller Harring   c) first footing

17 What gifts did the three kings bring to the infant Jesus? ▶

18 What plant do we kiss under at Christmas?

19 How many days does Lent last?

20 When do the English celebrate St George's day?

(1) What is the fastest four-legged animal?

(2) Which four-legged animal is called 'the ship of the desert'?

(3) What race did Red Rum win in 1973, 1974 and 1977?

(4) Which much-hunted animal is sometimes called *Reynard*?

(5) What creature brought the Black Death to Europe?

(6) What colour is a white rhinoceros?

(7) Which animal is the symbol of the World Wildlife Fund?

(8) What was the first animal to be domesticated by man?

(9) What animal spends most of its time hanging upside-down in trees?

(10) What's another name for the desert rat?

(11) What was the huge, hairy, prehistoric elephant called?

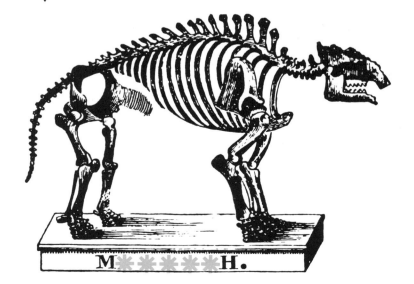

M******H.

12 Do badgers have tails?

13 Which animals build dams?

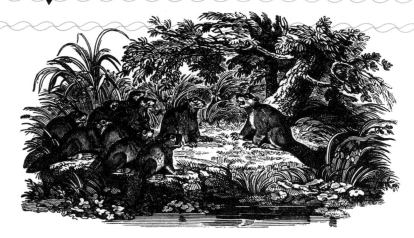

14 Does an otter eat fish or meat?

15 Which large dog takes its name from a saint?

16 What is the largest, land-living animal?

17 How many claws does a cat have on each of its front paws?

18 How many stomachs does a cow have?

19 What do elephants use their ears for, apart from fanning themselves and keeping flies at bay?

20 When running at maximum speed, which is quickest?
a) a horse   b) a wolf   c) a hare

21 Which common household pet sleeps on average for fourteen hours a day?

22 What did Robert Burns describe as wee, sleekit, cow'rin and tim'rous?

23 What do Europeans call the animal known as a moose in the Americas?

24 When a stoat turns white in winter, what does its name change to?

25 What's the collective word for a group of lions?

(1) Who was the first man to run the mile in less than four minutes?

(2) How many people are there in a 4 × 100 metres relay team? ▶

(3) How many miles are there in the marathon?

✓ ▼

▲

(4) Two of Britain's top male athletes share the initials S.C. Who are they?

(5) How heavy is the minimum weight of the shot in the shot put for men?
a) 16 lbs   b) 17 lbs   c) 18 lbs

(6) How many events are there in the pentathlon?

(7) What nationality was Zola Budd before she became British?

8   After which high-jumper is the Fosbury Flop named?

9   Who is Britain's top male decathlete?

10 How far did Yiannis Kouros run in 136 hours and 17 minutes in 1984?
    a) 750 kilometres   b) 1000 kilometres
    c) 1250 kilometres

11 What is the longest track event for men?

12 At what event does Fatima Whitbread excel?

13 What does AAA stand for?

14 How many lanes are there on a standard running track?

15 How many field events are there in the Olympics?

16 What is the maximum number of spikes on a standard running shoe?

17 What do the five rings of the Olympic flag represent?

18 Must a javelin stick in the ground for the throw to count?

19 What weighs 16 lbs (7.26 kb), is attached to a wire almost 4 ft (121.5 mm) long and is thrown at sports meetings?

20 Where were the first Olympic Games held for the disabled?

21 Which sort of jumping was once known as the hop, step and jump?

22 What is the shortest Olympic sprint distance?

23 Is there a pole-vaulting competition for women at the Olympics?

24 How many miles an hour would you have to run to average a four-minute mile?

25 When were the first Olympic Games held?
    a) 776 BC   b) 500 BC   c) 250 BC

(11) Which sea separates Japan from the mainland of Asia?
a) The Sea of Vladivostok   b) The Sea of Japan
c) The Korean Sea

(1) Which country's flag is made up of a red circle on a white background?

(2) Which famous Venetian merchant travelled to China in the thirteenth century?

(3) Which Chinese city has a Forbidden City within its boundaries?

(4) To which European country does Macao on the Chinese mainland belong?

(5) What is the only man-made object, it is said, that can be seen from the Moon?

(6) What mountain is sacred to the Japanese?

(7) Which colony will Britain give back to the Chinese in 1997?

(8) What is a kimono?
a) a Japanese robe   b) a Japanese tea ceremony
c) a Japanese bird

(9) Which tree gives its name to a pattern often seen on Japanese plates?

(10) Which Rodgers and Hammerstein musical tells the story of an Oriental king and a Welsh governess?

12 In which country was tea first grown commercially? ▼

17 What is the unit of currency in Japan? ✓

18 What is Bombay Duck made of?
a) duck b) fish c) chicken

19 Which Gilbert and Sullivan opera is set in Japan?

20 Which of the Tropics goes straight through southern China?

21 What material that originated in China do we get from *Bombyx mori* and *Antheraea mylitta*?

22 Japan has a famous kind of theatre. Is it
a) Yes or b) No?

✓ **23** Which British Queen had the same name as Hong Kong's capital?

24 What is *bonsai*?

✓ **25** Which Chinese city gave its name to kidnapping?

▲

13 Where did Chinese noblemen sometimes keep this small dog?

14 In which far-eastern country were US troops involved in a war during the 1960s and 1970s?

15 In which country could you watch this type of wrestling? ► ►
a) China b) Thailand c) Japan

16 From which oriental country did President Marcos flee in 1986?

1 One of the co-stars of *The Mosquito Coast* and *Stand By Me* is called
a) River Phoenix b) River Thames c) River Seine?

✓ **2** Who was paid a reputed $50 000 000 to endorse Pepsi Cola?

✓ **3** Which Beatle was gunned down in New York in 1980?

4 Who 'Sundanced' with Paul Newman and came 'Out of Africa' with Meryl Streep?
✓

▼

8 How does Miss Streisand spell her first name?
a) Barbra   b) Barbara   c) Babra

9 Ryan O'Neal's daughter is married to this tennis-playing 'Superbrat'. Who are they?

▼

✓ **5** Which superstar drives the Ratmobile?

6 Who starred in *Purple Rain*?

7 Which Bachelor Boy went on a Summer Holiday and had Time on his hands?

10) Today's young generation of Hollywood stars is called
a) The Ratpack b) The Bratpack c) The Flatpack?

11) What is Michael Jackson's middle name?

12) Which of the two Ronnies apologises too often?

13) Which movie actor did Madonna marry?

14) Harry Secombe, Peter Sellers and Spike Milligan all starred in a famous radio show. Was it
a) The Glums   b) The Goons   c) The Glooms?

15) Which US soap-opera star was a pupil at Britain's Royal Ballet School?
a) Joan Collins   b) Catherine Oxenberg   c) Emma Samms?

16) Who plays Mad Max in the *Mad Max* movies?

17) Which pop star appeared in the movie *Labyrinth*?

18) Who plays Superman on screen?

19) Before he became a star, was Harrison Ford a carpenter, an electrician or a plumber?

20) Which actor became Governor of California before moving on to greater things in 1980?

21) She's Australian; she's a housewife and she's a superstar. Who is she?

22) Kirk Douglas's son starred in the film *Romancing the Stone*. What's his first name?

23) Who wrote and directed the films *Manhattan, Hannah and her Sisters* and *Purple Rose of Cairo*?

24) Who starred in *The Color of Money* with Paul Newman?

25) The widow of which famous rock king stars in *Dallas*?

(4) American policemen ride Electra Glide bikes: who makes them?

(5) What part of a bicycle connects the crankset to the cogwheel?

(6) What would you be riding if you were 'walking the dog'?

(7) What colour are the fire-engines at most British airports?

(8) Silver Cloud and Silver Phantom are types of which make of car?

(9) What is the gear position called when a car is out of gear?

(10) How many wheels does a tandem have?

(1) What kind of bicycle did ET ride?

(2) What do you operate the gear lever with on a motor bike?

(3) What did the man who walked in front of early motor cars have to carry?

(11) When was the first fatal 'motor' accident?
a) 1832   b) 1842   c) 1852

(12) Which World War II villain encouraged Ferdinand Porsche to build the Volkswagen Beetle?

(13) What would you want if you asked the garage for an MOT?

(14) The world speed record for a car is
a) 1001 km/h   b) 1019 km/h   c) 1190 km/h?

(15) Which motor manufacturer produces a model called the Cherry?

(16) Which two cities are linked by the Orient Express?

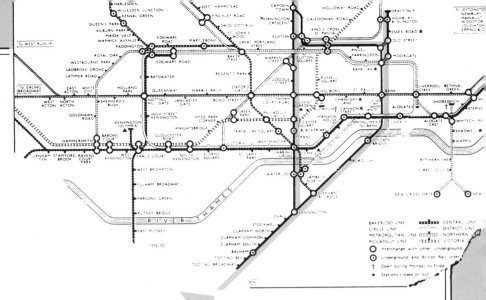

▲

17 Which train features in the title of an Andrew Lloyd Webber musical?

18 In which sport did Barry Sheen make his name?

19 What colour is the Northern Line on London Underground maps?
a) red   b) black   c) green

20 What make of car was turned into a time machine in *Back to the Future*?

✓ 21 What's a velodrome?

22 How do the Dukes of Hazzard get into their car?

23 What motorway would you go on to drive from London to Birmingham?

24 Where is the British Grand Prix held?

✓ 25 Who drives a red van in Greendale?

1. A person who is not what he appears to be is described as a wolf in ... what?

2. How many stitches does a stitch in time save?

3. How many swallows doth not a summer make?

4. 'One for sorrow: two for joy.' One what?

5. If you were on Shanks's Pony, how would you be travelling?

6. How many cooks spoil the broth?

7. If you lived in a glass house, what should you never throw?

8. Which emotion do you associate with green?

9. What do you bury when you make peace?

10. Who catches the worm?

11. Dead men don't tell what?

12. What is burning if someone is talking about you behind your back?

13. Who says 'What's up, Doc?'

14. If you marry in haste, what do you repent at?

15. Are church mice rich or poor?

16. What does a new broom sweep?

17. Where does the rain fall in Spain?

18. What did the church bells say to Dick Whittington?

▲

19 How many heads are better than one?

20 All that glitters is not what?

21 What kind of weather can you expect if there is red sky at night?

22 You may as well be hung for a sheep as a what?

23 If something is out of sight, what else is it out of?

24 Where is the grass greener?

25 What is a bird in the hand worth?

1. Mount Etna and Stromboli are both what?

2. Which west-coast US city was destroyed by an earthquake in 1906?

3. Surtsey, a volcanic island, appeared off the coast of which island country in 1963?
a) Tasmania   b) Iceland   c) Jersey

4. What do we call the molten rock that spews out of volcanoes? ▶ ▶

5. What is 1206 miles (1930 km) long, lies off the north-east coast of Australia and is made up of the skeletons of tiny sea creatures?

◀ ◀ ◀ 6. In which country are geysers a common sight?

7. Which famous waterfall lies between Lake Erie and Lake Ontario in North America?

8 Which river flows through the Grand Canyon?
a) The Rio Grande   b) The Colorado   c) The Gulf Stream

9 In which Middle Eastern sea is it almost impossible to sink?

10 If you saw a large, non-existent lake in the middle of a desert, what would you in fact be seeing?

11 Which country is famous for its fjords?

12 What is the world's highest mountain?

13 How much of the world's surface is covered in desert?
a) one eighth   b) one ninth   c) one tenth

14 Which of the world's lakes is the largest?

15 What is the largest island in the world?

16 Has anyone ever been killed by an earthquake in Britain?

17 What natural wonder may you see when the sun shines after the rain has passed over?

18 Has the temperature ever reached 100°F in Britain?

19 What kind of storms are traditionally given female Christian names?

20 What may happen after an underwater earthquake? ✓

21 In which mountain range would you find several of the highest peaks in the world?

22 What name did David Livingstone give to the falls he discovered in Africa in 1855?

▼

23 What colour are the cliffs of Dover?

24 What's the longest river in Britain?
a) the Thames   b) the Severn   c) the Tay

25 How old is the oldest plant in the world?
a) 11 700 years   b) 12 700 years   c) 13 700 years

1 Who was the first British ice-skater to win the Men's Ice Skating Olympic title?

2 Which Cliff was the 1981 Pot Black Champion?

3 How many gold medals did Mark Spitz win at the 1972 Olympics?
a) 5 b) 7 c) 9

4 What kind of fish is the heaviest ever caught by an angler?

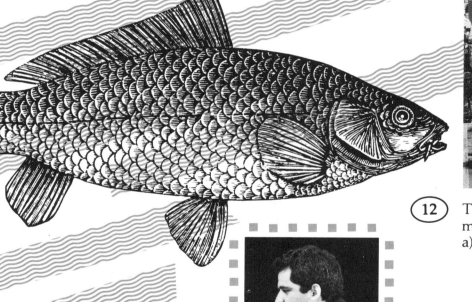

5 Gary Kasparov is the youngest men's world champion at which game?

6 What did Gary Sobers do in Glamorgan in 1968?

7 What world record, held by Bob Beamon since 1968, still stands?

8 In which sport is Willie Shoemaker an all-time champion?
a) gymnastics b) rugby c) horse racing

9 Who was the world's first heavyweight boxing champion?

10 Pam Shriver and her partner share the record for tennis Grand Slam doubles titles: who was her partner?

11 At which sport was Princess Anne European Champion?
▼

12 The maximum score for a three game ten-pin bowling match is 900. What's the world record?
a) 886 b) 890 c) 900

13 In which sport is the Champion Hurdle run?

14 Which ice-skaters hold the record for the most perfect 'sixes' while skating for one title?

15 Which golfer has won the US Masters golf championship more than any other?
a) Seve Ballesteros   b) Jack Nicklaus   c) Lee Trevino

16 What nationality is the Men's 200 metres champion, Alan Wells?

17 Which of these English cricketers achieved a record 100 centuries and 100 dismissals in 1986?

▼

18 Who has won the World Motor Racing Grand Prix Championship more than anyone else?

19 Which countries compete for the Rugby Union Five Nations Championship?

20 What is the world record British football pools payout?
a) £1 032 088   b) £1 117 890   c) £1 127 890

21 Which batsman has made more first-class centuries than any other?
a) Jack Hobbs   b) Leonard Hutton   c) Peter May

22 Rocky Marciano and Joe Louis were champions at which sport?

23 Is Louis Grenier a champion at darts, speed skating or billiards?

▲

24 Is champion tennis player Boris Becker right-handed or left-handed?

25 What's the heaviest weight lifted by a weightlifter in competition?
a) between 460–470 kg   b) between 470–480 kg
c) between 480–490 kg

1. Which canal connects the Atlantic and Pacific Oceans?

2. Which city is famous for its Golden Gate Bridge? ▶

3. How many Great Lakes are there?

4. The west coast of South America is dominated by which mountain range?

5. What is the capital of Cuba?

6. Simon Bolivar gave his name to which South American country?

7. What is the Americas' only 'big cat'?

8. On which day of the week are bullfights held in Mexico?

9. What language is most commonly spoken in South America?

10. How many stars are there on the US flag?

11. Which US states are separate from the others?

(12) In which state is Hollywood? ▶

(13) Which of the following is not a Canadian province?
a) Alberta   b) Victoria   c) Quebec

(14) The world's second-longest river is in South America: what is it?

(15) In which country did the Aztecs live?

(16) Kingston is the capital of which Caribbean country?

(17) What poles do American Indians carve with symbols and emblems?

(18) What is the nickname of the Royal Canadian Mounted Police?
▼

(19) The capital of Bolivia is the highest in the world: what's it called?

(20) Which Latin American country hosted the Olympics in 1976?

(21) Is a condor a bird, a river or a lake?

(22) The Straits of Magellan separate Tierra del Fuego from which South American country?

(23) The distance between North America and Asia is
a) 65 km   b) 650 km   c) 6500 km?

▲
(24) What spitting animal is a native of Peru?

(25) What are Princeton, Harvard and Yale?

1. Where would you find Brainless?

2. Who is the 'short-sighted gink' in the *Beezer*?

3. Which Scottish comic character sits on a bucket?

4. What kind of animal is Fred Basset?

5. Which cat lives with his creator Jim Davies?

6. Which comic does Smasher appear in?

7. What's the big bird in Sesame Street called?

8. Who is Slippy?

9. The *Dandy* has two desperate characters: who are they?

10. Which comic strip hero is also known as Clark Kent?

11. Who did Peter Parker turn into after he was bitten by a spider?

12. Who is Batman's assistant?

▼

13. What does Lord Snooty wear on his head?

14. Who sleeps on top of his kennel?

15. Who is *Topper's* 'tricky' character?

▲

16. What sort of animal is Roland Rat's friend Kevin?

17. What is the name of Tintin's dog?

▶

18 Which muppet is in love with Kermit?

19 Whose enemy is Ming the Merciless?

▼

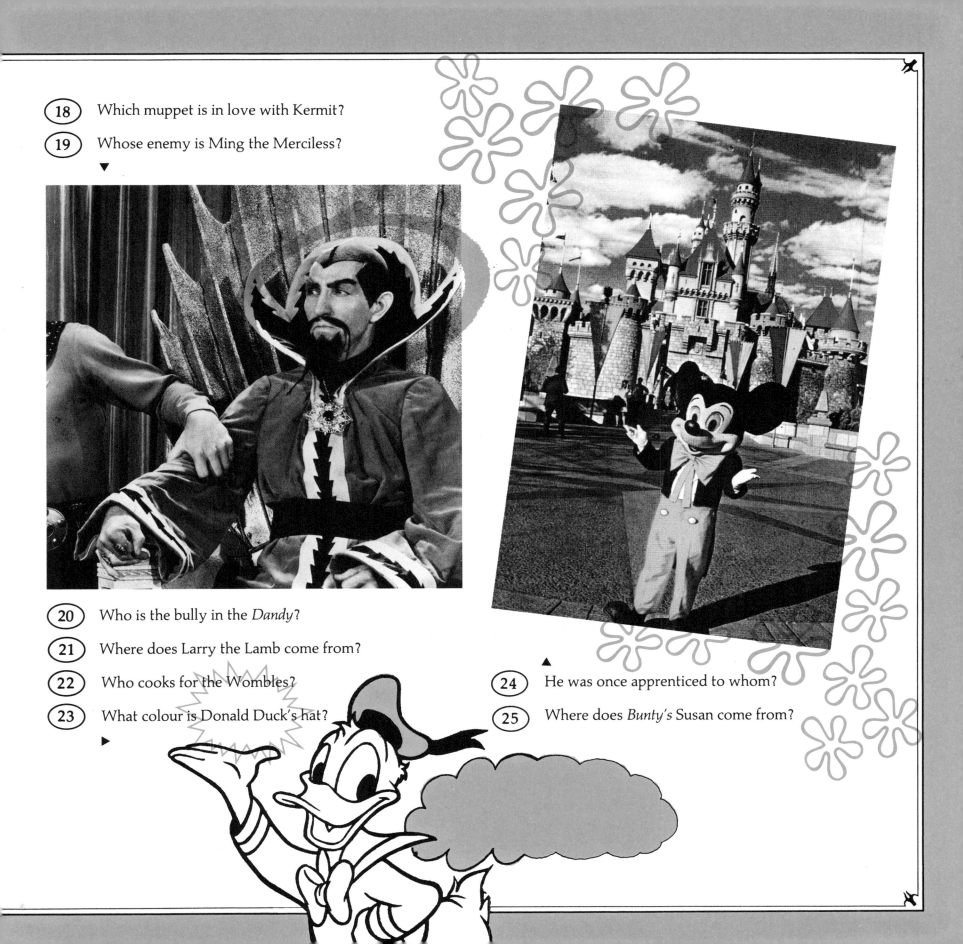

20 Who is the bully in the *Dandy*?

21 Where does Larry the Lamb come from?

22 Who cooks for the Wombles?

23 What colour is Donald Duck's hat?

▶

▲

24 He was once apprenticed to whom?

25 Where does *Bunty's* Susan come from?

1. What's the opposite of an alkali?

2. Why is aluminium foil sometimes put between the walls in new houses?

3. Why do electricians wear rubber gloves when they are working?

4. What is the chemical symbol for hydrogen?
   a) H   b) Hn   c) Hy

5. What happens to water at 100°C?

6. Which travels faster, light waves or sound waves?

7. How many colours are there in a rainbow?

8. In which direction does a compass needle point when it settles? ▶

9. AC stands for alternating current. What does DC stand for?
   a) direct current   b) distorted current   c) diamolic current

10. Is glass the only material used to make lenses in a pair of glasses?

▼

11. Does a craniologist study the skull, the eyes or birds? ▶

12. Does a convex lens curve inwards or outwards?

13. What is detergent used for dispersing at sea?

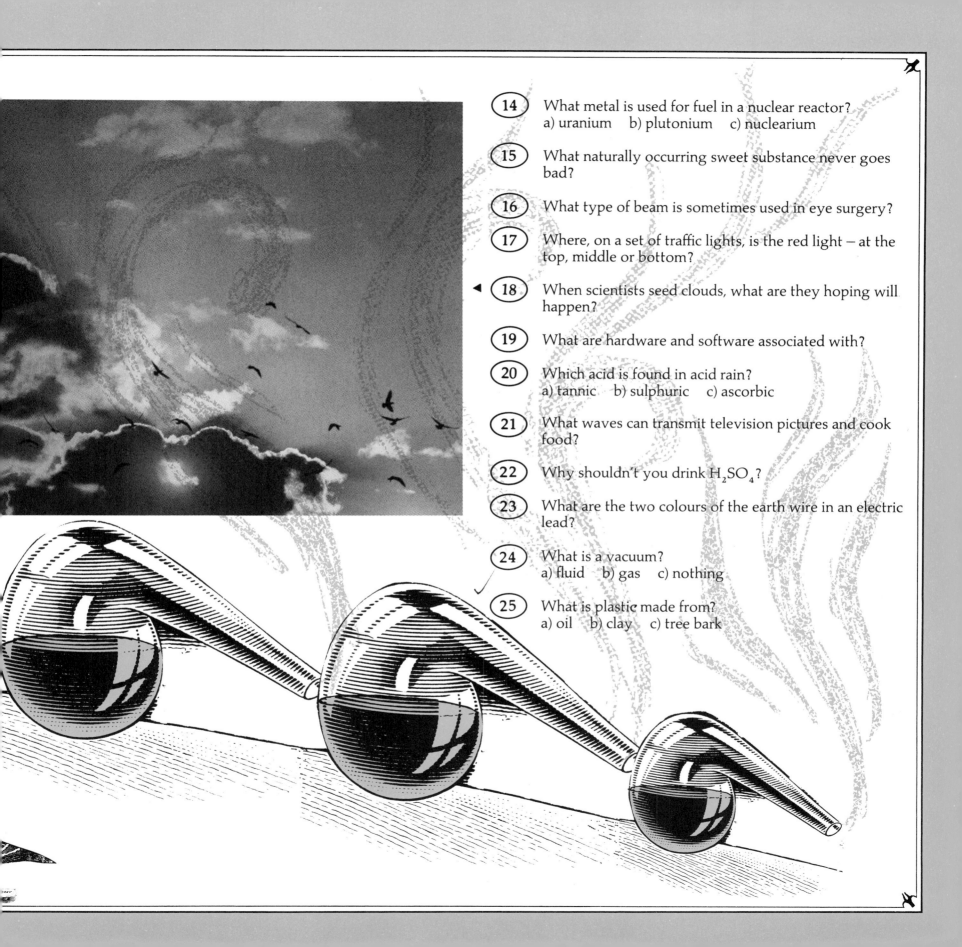

14) What metal is used for fuel in a nuclear reactor?
a) uranium   b) plutonium   c) nuclearium

15) What naturally occurring sweet substance never goes bad?

16) What type of beam is sometimes used in eye surgery?

17) Where, on a set of traffic lights, is the red light — at the top, middle or bottom?

◄ 18) When scientists seed clouds, what are they hoping will happen?

19) What are hardware and software associated with?

20) Which acid is found in acid rain?
a) tannic   b) sulphuric   c) ascorbic

21) What waves can transmit television pictures and cook food?

22) Why shouldn't you drink H_2SO_4?

23) What are the two colours of the earth wire in an electric lead?

24) What is a vacuum?
a) fluid   b) gas   c) nothing

25) What is plastic made from?
a) oil   b) clay   c) tree bark

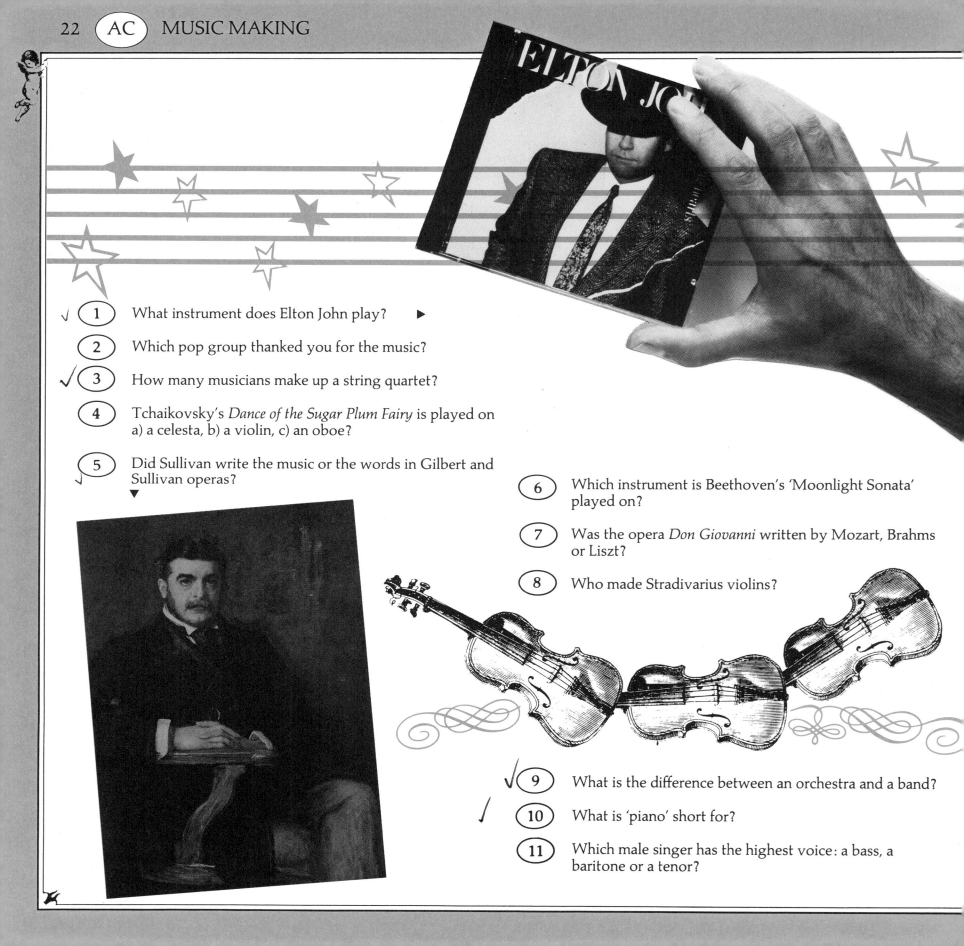

1. What instrument does Elton John play? ▶

2. Which pop group thanked you for the music?

3. How many musicians make up a string quartet?

4. Tchaikovsky's *Dance of the Sugar Plum Fairy* is played on
a) a celesta, b) a violin, c) an oboe?

5. Did Sullivan write the music or the words in Gilbert and
Sullivan operas?
▼

6. Which instrument is Beethoven's 'Moonlight Sonata'
played on?

7. Was the opera *Don Giovanni* written by Mozart, Brahms
or Liszt?

8. Who made Stradivarius violins?

9. What is the difference between an orchestra and a band?

10. What is 'piano' short for?

11. Which male singer has the highest voice: a bass, a
baritone or a tenor?

15. Which musical instrument traditionally accompanies flamenco dancing?

16. Which instrument does James Galway play?

17. In the world of hi-fi, what does CD stand for?

18. Who is the patron saint of music?

19. For whom are Requiem Masses sung?

20. Who wrote the symphonies called *The Pastoral, Eroica* and *The Fifth*?

12. Who was the tympanist in The Beatles?

13. What colourful Rhapsody did George Gershwin write?

14. When Torvill and Dean won their last title, what music did they skate to?
a) Barnum   b) Mack and Mabel   c) Ravel's Bolero

21. Which of these stringed instruments is the biggest?
a) a violin   b) a double bass   c) a cello

22. What sort of music did Johann Strauss write?

23. From which country did the didgeridoo come?

24. Who was the music maker in Robin Hood's band of merry men?

25. What is the largest musical instrument?

◄ (1) Do cacti store water in their needles, their stems or their roots?

(2) What is a yam?

(3) What kind of fruit is sold in hands?

✓ (4) What colour is a tulip's stem?

(5) Is the tomato a fruit, a vegetable or a bulb?
▼

(6) What is a prune?

(7) Is the water melon a fruit?

(8) Brandy is made from the fruit of which plant? ►

(9) Do peanuts grow above or below ground?

(10) Which trees grow from acorns?

(15) Cos and Icebergs are types of what?

(16) Where would you find sepals?

(17) Plants grow towards light. Is this
a) heliotropism   b) photosynthesis   c) aquatropism?

(18) What busy flower is correctly called *Impatiens wallerana*?

(19) Which plant gives off gas?
a) the gas plant   b) the butane plant   c) the calor plant

(20) What fungus could you fry for breakfast?

(21) There's a music hall song about a big plant. Is it
a) The Biggest Aspidistra   b) The Biggest
Polyanthus   c) The Biggest Busy Lizzie . . . . in the
World?

(22) What part of a plant gives off oxygen?

(23) Maidenhair, Boston, asparagus and hart's tongue are all
what type of plant?

(24) What do we call the fruit of the bramble?

(25) What part of the flower bears the pollen?

(11) Is the outer layer of bark on a tree dead or alive?

(12) What fruit is a sultana?

(13) Does rubber come from trees, flowers or bushes?

(14) What type of pear is the main ingredient of the Mexican
dish *guacamole*?

1. Which organization did William Smith found in 1883?

2. What is the NSPCC concerned with?

3. Does London Scottish play rugby at Richmond, Twickenham or Putney?

4. What does RoSPA try to prevent?

5. Which club did Boy George belong to?

6. Which organization is said to be concerned with 'Jam and Jerusalem'?
   a) The Women's Institute   b) The Boy Scouts
   c) The Jewish Confectioner's Society

7. What do the letters RSPCA stand for?

8. Who is the president of The Girl Guides?

9. This has been described as 'The best club in London'? Is it a) The House of Commons   b) The Church of England   c) The House of Lords

10. What does YMCA stand for?

11. What would you see at the NFT?
    a) needlework   b) films   c) trains

12 Where are the headquarters of the Zoological Society of London?

13 If you belonged to the RSPB, what would your hobby be?

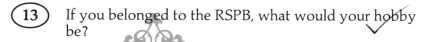

14 Which of Lord Baden-Powell's organizations can you join at the age of eleven?

15 Whose motto is 'Good Companions, Good Countrymen, Good Citizens'?
a) The Young Farmers   b) The Woodland Folk
c) The Archers

16 What is the junior branch of the Girl Guides called?

17 Who 'Dib Dib Dib Woofs'?

18 Which organization's motto is *Be Prepared*?

19 Which ambulance brigade attends sporting events in this country?

20 What is the RSC involved with?
a) motoring   b) cats   c) theatre

21 What are members of the Society of Jesus better known as?

22 Of which society were William, Ginger, Henry and Douglas members?

23 Who do the AA and RAC assist in times of difficulties?

24 Where does the All England Lawn Tennis and Croquet Club have its headquarters?
a) Queens   b) Wimbledon   c) Hurlingham

25 Of which society, granted a Royal Charter by Charles II, were Christopher Wren and Isaac Newton presidents?
a) The Royal Society   b) The Co-op   c) The Friendly Society

1. What is the capital of Australia?
2. What kind of settlement did the British establish at Botany Bay?
3. What was the name of Captain Cook's ship?
4. What kind of animal is a kangaroo? ▼

5. What name was given to the original inhabitants of Australia?
6. Which island is separated from the Australian mainland by the Bass Strait?
7. New Zealand is divided into two main islands: what are they called?
8. Which bird is the symbol of New Zealand? ▼

9. What nickname is given to the New Zealand Rugby team?
10. What is the capital of New South Wales?
11. Which Territory is one of the six states of Australia?
12. Dunedin in New Zealand is named after which Scottish city?
13. Which Australian actor played Crocodile Dundee? ▶ ▶ ▶
14. Which Ned was a famous Australian outlaw?

15 Australia has a famous rock: what is it called?

16 What are the wild dogs of Australia called?

17 Which famous New Zealander climbed Everest in 1953?

18 Which ocean lies off the west coast of Australia?

19 What is this large Australian bird?

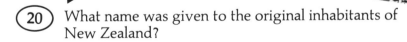

20 What name was given to the original inhabitants of New Zealand?

21 What is the longest river in Australia?

22 New Zealand's highest mountain is named after the man who discovered Australia: what is it called?

✓ **23** What kind of bears live in Australia?

24 What is the most important farm animal in Australia and New Zealand?

25 How far is Australia from New Zealand?
a) 1900 miles   b) 1930 miles   c) 1950 miles.

1. Is Norway a member of the Common Market?

2. In which Middle Eastern country was Terry Waite taken hostage in 1987?

3. Who has been head of Cuba since 1959?
   a) Fidel Castro   b) Che Guevara   c) General Galtieri

4. What are the two major political parties in the USA?

5. What does SALT stand for?
   a) Strategic Arms Limitation Talks   b) Southern Armies' Land Tanks   c) Stray Animals' Litter Trays

6. What are the Liberal Party and the SDP jointly known as?

7. What nationality is the present Pope?
   ▼

8. Are women allowed to be priests in the Church of England?

9. Which country is led by the Ayatollah Khomeini?

10. What is Mrs Thatcher's husband's first name?

11. He owns an airline, a record company and the full-scale version of the power-boat he's holding. Who is he?
    ▼

12. Which member of Duran Duran was involved in a yachting accident?

13. What is the *Mail on Sunday*'s colour magazine called?
    a) *You*   b) *Sunday*   c) *The Letter*

14. What does RUC stand for?

15. *The Herald of Free Enterprise* sank in 1987. Did the tragedy occur
    a) off Calais   b) off Dunkirk   c) off Zeebrugge?

16 Wendy Dagworthy, Katherine Hamnet and the Emanuels are all what?

17 Who is the leader of the British Labour Party?

18 Which Rolling Stone's girl friend is the model, Jerry Hall?

19 Who was the second member of the royal family to visit China on an official visit?

20 Who is the present Archbishop of Canterbury?
▼

24 What tax is added to many goods and services in the United Kingdom?

25 Which branch of the Armed Services did Prince Edward quit in 1987?
✓ ▼

21 What was the Princess of Wales's name before she married Prince Charles? ▶

22 Who lives in Number 11 Downing Street?
a) The Chancellor of the Exchequer   b) The Lord Chancellor   c) The Chancellor of the University of Oxford.

23 Is the Booker Prize awarded for the best novel published in Britain in the year, the best speech or the best television commercial?

1. What unit of measurement did Henry I define as the distance from the tip of his nose to his thumb?

2. How many furlongs are there in a mile?

3. How many millimetres are there to an inch?

4. What system of measurement was introduced during the French Revolution?

5. How many thousands make up one million?

6. What is 0°C equal to on the Fahrenheit scale?

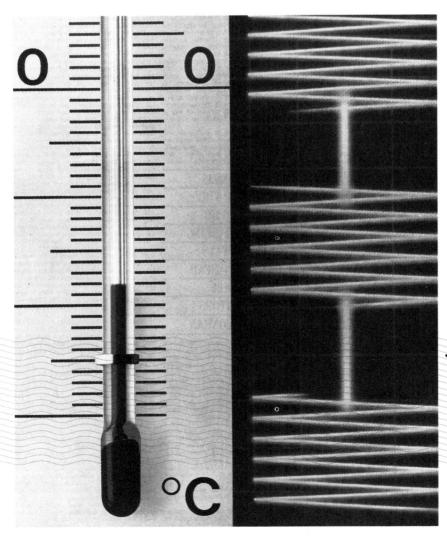

7. What number do Julian, Dick, Anne, George and Timmy make up?

8. What is the Imperial equivalent of 1.61 kilometres?

9. How many days are there in a leap year?

10. What do we measure in carats?

11. Which is heavier, a kilo of coal or a kilo of feathers?

12. What are there 525 600 of in a year?

13. How long is a lunar month?

14. What is the measurement cc an abbreviation of?

There came a little blackbird,
And nipp'd off her nose.

(20) What does the abbreviation mph stand for?

✓(21) What are millibars?

(22) If you were on a diet, what would you be counting?

▲

(23) How many loaves are there in a baker's dozen?

(24) How many days are there in the month of October?

(25) How many witches did Macbeth meet?

▲

(15) How many blackbirds were baked in a pie according to the nursery rhyme?

(16) 727, 737 and 747 are all types of what?

(17) What is measured in decibels and phons?

(18) Which book contains 66 separate books and 3 566 480 letters?

(19) How many deadly sins are there? ▶

(1) Which screen villain is played by actor Larry Hagman?

(2) What kind of companies are Russia's Kirov and Bolshoi?

(3) Which Hollywood star appears with an orang-utan called Clyde?

(4) Who set T.S. Eliot's poems to music for the show *Cats*?

(5) In which 'End' would you find many of London's theatres?

(6) What is the name of Kermit's bear friend?

(7) Which Russian ballet star starred in *The Turning Point* and *White Nights*?

(10) Which of the following has never played James Bond?
a) David Niven   b) Sean Connery   c) Roger Moore
d) Michael Caine

(11) What was the name of the Wookie in *Star Wars*?

(12) What statues do the American Film Academy award each year?

(8) Of which stage organization is Prince Edward patron?

(9) Which Li'l orphan girl started as a cartoon heroine before going on stage and finishing up on the screen?

13 Which famous teenage diarist appeared on stage in London and in a television series?

14 Which 'gangster' movie had a cast of children?
▼

15 Which Charles Dickens' novel is the film *Oliver* based on?

16 Which stage musical tells the story of American showman Phineas Taylor Barnum?
a) *Phineas' Rainbow*   b) *Barnum*   c) *Circus Boy*

17 Which fairy-tale character is the heroine of the opera *La Cenerentola*?

18 What was the Pink Panther in the Pink Panther films?
▼

19 If you were a 'trekky' which television series would you be addicted to?

20 What was the title of Madonna's first film?

◄ **21** Which movie and TV series was set in a New York stage school?

22 According to superstition, what should you never do in an actor's dressing room?
a) whistle   b) click your fingers   c) cut your fingernails

23 What was the sequel to *Raiders of the Lost Ark*?

24 For which role did Julie Andrews win an Oscar?

25 What is the longest-running play on the London stage?

1. Which jungle character was created by Edgar Rice Burroughs?

2. Do flying squirrels fly like birds?

3. One kind of forest is deciduous: what is the other type known as?

4. How many humps does a dromedary have?

5. Are there lions living wild in India?

6. On which large island are lemurs found?
   a) Madagascar   b) Sri Lanka   c) Tasmania

7. Can leopards climb trees?

8. What is the most common plant in the desert?

9. How does a rattlesnake announce its presence?

10. What kind of tree does a koala bear feed on?

11. What is the average rainfall in the desert?
    a) less than five inches a year   b) between five and ten inches a year   c) more than ten inches a year.

12. On either side of which line would you find tropical rain forest?

13. In which forest did Robin Hood live?

14. Many desert animals hunt at night: are they nocturnal or diurnal?

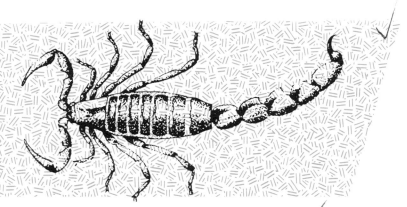

15 Where would you find a scorpion's sting? ✓

16 How many species of trees grow in the Amazon jungle?
a) around 500   b) around 1000   c) around 2500

17 Which desert creature leaves its tail behind when running from danger? ✓

18 On which sort of tree would you be most likely to see a pine marten?

19 Are more coniferous forests found north or south of the Equator?

20 What does a camel store in its hump?
a) water   b) fat   c) nothing
▼

21 Which carniverous cat lives in the forests of Canada?

22 Does this animal sleep in dens on the ground or in nests in trees?
▼

23 Can you ever see flowers in the desert?

24 What are rain forests also known as?

25 Which American 'big cat' lives in the jungles of South America?

1. In what year did England win the World Cup?

2. The Saint and who preview Saturday soccer on ITV? ▶

3. Which football club plays at Rugby Park?

4. Which king banned football in the City of London?
   a) Edward II   b) Henry VIII   c) George VI

5. Which is the oldest club in the Football League?

6. Which was the first British club to win the European Champion Clubs Cup?

7. How many countries have won the World Cup three times?

8. These two brothers played in England's World-Cup winning team. Who are they?
   ▶

9 The highest recorded football crowd is
   a) 205 000   b) 210 000   c) 220 000?

10 Who used his hands to score a vital goal against
   England in the 1986 World Cup?

11 What colour is the England team strip?

12 How long is each 'half' in a game of soccer?

13 The most postponed soccer game was postponed how
   many times?
   a) 19   b) 29   c 39

14 Who is Edson Arantes do Nascimento better known as? ▶

15 Who is the manager of England's soccer team?

16 Merseyside boasts two first-division soccer clubs. One
   is Liverpool, what is the other one?

17 Which newspaper sponsors the English League?

18 What sort of football is played with fifteen men in each
   side, and a ball that tapers to a point at either end?

19 Which London club does Charlie Nicholas play for?

20 Which club is known as 'Spurs'?

21 When was the first World Cup held?

22 What does FIFA stand for?

23 How wide are the goals in soccer?
   a) 20 feet   b) 24 feet   c) 28 feet

24 If a player is substituted during a game of soccer, can he
   return to the field?

25 To what pressure should a soccer ball be inflated at the
   start of a match?
   a) 10 lbs/sq. in.   b) 15 lbs/sq. in.   c) 20 lb/sq. in.

(1) Where are the headquarters of the European Economic Community?

(2) In which European capital would you be if you were strolling along the *Champs Elysées*? ▶

(3) Which was the last western European country to host the Olympics?

(4) Where would you see sea-walls called dykes?

(5) In which hills does this river have its source? ▼

(6) Where is the Matterhorn?

(7) Bullfighting is a popular sport in which European ▶ country?

(8) Which river is known as the Dunaj in Czechoslovakia and the Duna in Hungary?

(9) West Berlin is surrounded by which country?

(10) With how many countries does Switzerland share its borders?

(11) Where is the Côte d'Azur?

(12) Which two countries share Cyprus?

(13) What stretch of water do you cross to go from Dover to Cherbourg?

(14) What is the smallest country in Europe?

(15) What do the initials GDR stand for?

(16) If you were spending pesetas, which country would you be in?

(17) Not counting USSR and Turkey, how many countries are there in Europe? ▶

(18) Herm and Sark belong to which group of islands?

(22) The Tyrrhenian Sea separates Italy from which island?

(23) What is Europe's longest river?

(24) Vaduz is the capital of which tiny European country?

(25) The Pyrenees separates France from which country?

▲

(19) Where would you see this building?

(20) The Algarve is in which European country?

(21) Which country owns the Faeroe Islands?

1 Which TV magician says 'Not a lot' a lot?

2 What would you be watching if you were at a *son et lumière* show?

3 Which entertainer partnered Ernie Wise for many years?

4 Why does the Queen or other members of the Royal Family go to the London Palladium or the Theatre Royal, Drury Lane every November?

5 How would someone versed in the 'art of terpsichore' entertain you?

6 Which female entertainer was a pop singer for many years and now surprises us a lot on television?

7 Which ex-newsreader presents *The Clothes Show*?

8 Which superstar rodent was discovered by Breakfast TV?

9 What is a cabaret?

10 Marcel Marceau is famous the world over, but he never says a word. How does he entertain us?

11 What is a marionette better known as?

12 Who was responsible for the films *Cinderella, Sleeping Beauty* and *Fantasia*?

13 Which US president was shot while he was in the theatre?

(14) Fred Astaire and Ginger Rogers entertained our parents in films of the 1930s and 1940s. What were they especially good at?

(15) If you were invited to a masked ball what would you have to wear?

(16) What did the film *That's Entertainment* celebrate?
a) Circus   b) The Hollywood Musical   c) Ballet

(17) How did Harry Houdini entertain audiences at the beginning of this century?

(18) What do Lambchop and Sooty have in common?

(19) What is the Christian name of the actor Lord Olivier?
▼

(20) What sort of entertainer is Dominique Devereux in *The Colbys* and *Dynasty*?

(21) Which 'everyday story of farming folk' has been on Radio 4 for many years?

(22) What entertainers are good at prestidigitation?

(23) What kind of entertainer is Bobby Davro? ►
a) a singer   b) an impressionist   c) a dancer

(24) How did troubadours entertain people in medieval times?

(25) Scott Joplin wrote *The Entertainer*: is it
a) a piece of music   b) a book or   c) a play?

9 Which country does a car displaying the letter D come from?

10 D-type, E-type and S-type are all makes of which car?

11 Who went to sea in a beautiful pea-green boat?

12 What are canal long-boats more familiarly known as?

13 Which motorway circles London?

14 What would you do with a junk – sail it, pedal it or fly it?

15 What would you be travelling on if you were going down the Cresta Run?

16 What did the Wright Brothers do at Kitty Hawk on December 17, 1903?
▶

1 What is the only commercial supersonic airliner?

2 By what name is the liner *Queen Elizabeth II* better known?

3 What was the world's first nuclear submarine?

4 Which duke gave his name to Britain's first canal?

5 What were tea clippers?

6 Which city had the world's first underground railway system?

7 Where is Grand Central Station?

8 What colour were Model T Fords?   ▶ ▶ ▶

17 If you were travelling at Mach 2, what speed would you be travelling at?

18 What were *Graf Zeppelin* and the *Hindenburg*?

19 What is a dhow?

◀ **20** For what kind of transport is San Francisco famous?

21 What pulls a rickshaw?
a) an ox   b) a cart horse   c) a man

✓ **22** What is the Royal Yacht called?

23 The Paris Underground is called
a) The Metro   b) L'Underground   c) La sous-terre?

▼ **24** In which ship did the Pilgrim Fathers sail to the New World?

25 What is France's major airline called?

1 'Peeping' who peeped at Lady Godiva as she rode through the streets of Coventry?

2 What word came into the language when people refused to talk to Captain Boycott?

3 What French phrase do we use for high fashion?
a) *Haute cuisine*   b) *Haute couture*   c) *Haute coiffure*

4 What word can mean a school teacher or captain of a ship?

5 If a woman was made a Dame of the Order of the British Empire, what letters would she put after her name?

6 If a Cockney was talking about his 'trouble and strife' what would he be talking about?

7 What does SWALK mean if you print it on the back of an envelope?

8 Whose motto is *Dieu et mon Droit*?
▼

9 You have five seconds to answer this. What is the twelfth letter of the alphabet?

10 What is the last letter of the Greek alphabet that is also the name of a make of watch?
▼

11 What English phrase do the French use for 'the weekend'?

12 Who is the 'PM'?

13 What sign did Sir Winston Churchill use as a symbol during the war?
▼

23 Is the letter O a vowel or a consonant?

24 BEA and BOAC combined to form BA. What do these letters stand for?

25 What is special about the word 'rhythms'?

14 Who was James Bond's boss?

15 What does rsvp stand for?

16 Which Dickens' character became used as a word for a miser? ▶

17 What do the initials QC stand for?

18 What were the letters L, s and d the signs for?

19 What is Sanskrit?

20 What does 'Mac' mean in names such as Macdonald and MacKay?

21 What word makes you yawn when you read it?

22 LMS and LNER were both what?

(1) Which direction is opposite north-east? ✓

(2) What do we call the chunks of ice that break off from the ice caps and float in the oceans? ▼

(3) Which stream of warm water washes part of the west coast of the British Isles? ✓

(4) What is meteorology?
a) the study of weather b) the study of space meteors
c) The study of measurement

(5) Which natural rock was once written on by schoolchildren instead of paper? ✓

(6) What always precedes a clap of thunder?

(7) What does the Earth do every 23 hours 56 minutes and 4 seconds?

✓ (8) What type of rock are the White Cliffs of Dover made of ?

(9) What is naturally stored in artesian wells?

(10) Do glaciers ascend or descend a mountain? ▼

(11) What is the mountain range that runs from Alaska to Mexico called?
a) The Rockies   b) The Andes   c) The Sierra Nevada

(12) Do stalactites grow up or down? ▶ ▶ ▶

13) Does amber come from trees, mines or the sea?

14) Where would you find an atoll? ✓

15) Where is the Grand Canyon? ▶

16) ✓ What three-sided nut shares its name with a South American country?

17) What are the Gobi, Great Sand and Sahara all types of?

18) Which of the following is not transparent?
a) emerald   b) opal   c) topaz

19) What are cumulus, stratus and nimbus types of?

✓ 20) Are there fleas in the Arctic?

21) Would you find a plateau on high land or low land?

22) What kind of volcano is no longer dangerous?

23) Is turpentine obtained from coal, oil or trees?

✓ 24) What colour is jade?

✓ 25) What point would you climb to if you wanted to breathe the thinnest air?

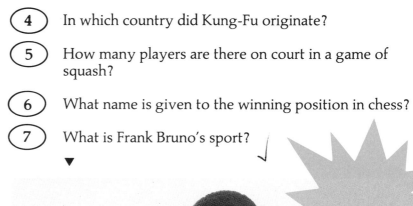

4. In which country did Kung-Fu originate?

5. How many players are there on court in a game of squash?

6. What name is given to the winning position in chess?

7. What is Frank Bruno's sport?

1. What dangerous martial art has a name meaning 'empty hand' in Japanese?

2. In which sport would you use an epée, foil and sabre?

3. Who beat Kevin Curren to become the youngest Men's Singles Wimbledon champion?

8 In which sport was Giant Haystack a great favourite?

9 What's the heaviest weight in professional boxing?

10 What nationality is squash champion Jahangir Khan?
▼

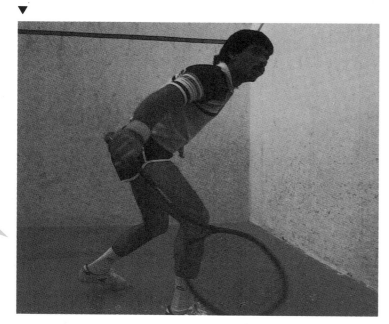

11 How many black squares are there on a draughts board?

12 In conkers, what does a tenner become when it beats a fiver?

13 What boxer boasted that he 'floats like a butterfly, stings like a bee'?

14 What gambling game has a croupier spinning a wheel?

15 How many Scrabble pieces do you put in your rack at the start of a game?

16 What game is played with the lightest ball?

17 Who was the youngest player to win a match at Wimbledon?
a) Tracy Austin   b) Andrea Jaeger   c) Kathy Rinaldi

18 What do you land on that sends you backwards in a game of Snakes and Ladders?

19 How many squares are there in a game of noughts and crosses?

20 Not counting the reds and the white, how many coloured balls are there in a game of snooker?

21 What nationality is this golfer?
▼

22 What game has versions called shanghai, cricket and round the clock?

23 What sportsman uses a ball marker before picking his ball off the ground?

24 What keeps a Frisbee stable during flight?
a) its speed   b) its spin   c) its weight

25 What would you lose if you are unlucky at Russian Roulette?

1. Where would you see Sugar Loaf Mountain?

2. Wall Street and Fifth Avenue are thoroughfares in which American city?

3. Where would you see the Swiss Guard? ▼

4. Which famous Australian harbour has a well-known bridge and opera house a short distance from each other?

5. Where in the world might you travel in a gondola on a canal? ▶

6. Where would you most likely waltz to the music of the Strauss family?

7. If you weren't in an airplane, but were 29 029 feet above sea level, where would you be?

8. Where could you see the mummified corpse of Lenin? ▼

(9) Where did the Phantom of the Opera live?

(10) In which ocean are the West Indies?

(11) Where could you see the last of the Seven Wonders of the World?

(12) Where do the Queen and members of her family spend Christmas?

(13) Where would you drive on an *autostrada*?

(14) The capital of Brazil is Brazilia. What's the largest city?
a) Brazilia   b) Sao Paulo   c) Rio de Janeiro

(15) Zanzibar and Tanganyika, combined in 1964 to form which modern African state?

(16) Is Belgium a kingdom, a republic or a grand duchy?

(17) Of which African state is Djibouti the capital?

(18) Which two countries are divided by Hadrian's Wall?

(19) In which country would you see The Valley of the Kings?

(20) Washington D.C. is the capital of the United States. What does D.C. stand for?

(21) In which country would you find the spectacular Taj Mahal?

(22) In which city is this famous gate?
▼

(23) Of which country is Greenland a part?

(24) Which Greek hero shares his name with a European capital?

(25) Krung Thep is the capital of Thailand: what is it better known as?

3 What comes in skimmed, long-life and pasteurised varieties?

4 What are pecans, pistachios and almonds?

5 Which popular drink was first sold in 1886?
▼

1 What number appears on Heinz tins?

2 Which brown sauce has a picture of this building on it?
▼

6 Which fish does caviar come from?

✓ (7) What do we traditionally eat on Shrove Tuesday?

✓ (8) Which animal gives us mutton?

(9) What flavour was the first-ever soup by Campbells?

(10) What is the Italian word for pie? ✓
▼

(11) ✓ Which vitamin are oranges rich in?

(12) What are Darjeeling, Earl Grey and Lapsang Souchong types of?

(13) What was Miss Muffet eating when the spider ▶ frightened her?

(14) If you were eating Szechuan, Cantonese or Huaiyang, in what country would you be?

(15) What pudding is named after a cold American state?

(16) What country does haggis come from?

(17) What plant do we derive chocolate from?

(18) What does decaffeinated coffee lack?

(19) What are 'Big Macs' and 'Half-pounders'?

(20) What is the staple food in Asia?

(21) If you were munching a Granny Smith, what would you be eating?

(22) What do you mix to make shandy?

(23) What kind of fish is a kipper?

(24) Peach Melba is named after
a) Melba St John   b) Nellie Melba   c) Peaches Patterson?

(25) What does the French word *gateau* mean?

① Where was Neil Armstrong when he said 'This is one small step for a man, but a giant leap for mankind'?

② What is the farthest planet from the Sun?

③ Which planet is named after the Goddess of Love?

④ In which galaxy is the Sun?

⑤ What was the first space satellite called?

⑥ Which US president was Cape Canaveral named after for a short time?

⑦ What TV programme does this man present?

▼

⑩ Is Halley's Comet the brightest ever seen?

⑪ Which Walt Disney character shares his name with a planet?

⑫ How far is the Moon from the Earth? ▶
a) 230 000 miles   b) 240 000 miles   c) 250 000 miles

⑧ How did Yuri Gagarin, the first man in space, die?
a) in a car crash   b) in a plane crash   c) in a rocket crash

⑨ Who is the captain of the starship *Enterprise* in *Star Trek*? ▶

(13) Which TV Time Lord travels in a Tardis?

(14) What is Alpha Centauri?

(15) The first animal to travel in space was called Leika: was she a dog, a donkey or a rabbit?

(16) Which planet did Superman come from?

(17) What are Sagittarius, Scorpio and Aries?

(18) After whom is the famous Comet named?
a) Edmund Halley   b) Bill Haley   c) Mary Haley Bell

(19) When there is an eclipse of the Sun, is the Earth between the Sun and the Moon, is the Moon between the Sun and the Earth or is the Sun between the Moon and the Earth?

(20) What nationality was the first woman in space?

(21) Which TV programme features Pigs in Space?

(22) The National Aeronautics and Space Administration is better known as what?

(23) What happened to the American Space Shuttle *Challenger* in 1986?

(24) What is Ursa Major better known as?

(25) On a clear night, how many stars are visible to the naked eye?
a) 2000   b) 3000   c) 4000

(1) What, according to legend, did St George slay?

(2) What bird rose from its own ashes?

▼

(3) Where did King Arthur and his knights live?

▼

(4) Which god is Thursday named after?

(5) Which bird picked a thorn from Christ's crown?

(6) Who is the Patron Saint of Greece and Scotland?

(7) Who ran off with Paris, so starting the Trojan Wars?

✓ (8) What should you never look at through glass?

✓ (9) Which firework is named after a saint?

(10) What kind of bird sat on Merlin's shoulder?

▼

MERLIN

(11) Who was the most important god for the Romans?

(12) Who sailed in search of the Golden Fleece?

(13) Who had snakes in her hair and turned anyone who looked at her into stone?

(14) Why were sailors afraid of the sirens?

(15) How many labours was Hercules forced to perform?

16 What was the only part of Achilles' body that was vulnerable?

17 Robert Fitzooth, Earl of Huntingdon, is better known as whom?

▼

18 If it rains on St Swithin's Day, how many more days of rain can we expect?

19 Who, according to legend, nodded off in the Kaatskill Mountains and wakened twenty years later?

20 How did Greek soldiers enter Troy?

21 Who did the Lady of Shalott fall in love with? ▶

22 Who flew too close to the Sun and fell into the sea when the wax on his wings melted?

23 Which mythical animal has a lion's tail, a horse's body and a single horn on its head?

24 Romeo's last name was Montague: what was Juliet's?

25 Which legendary city did Sir Walter Raleigh go in search of?

▼

1. How many leagues under the sea did Jules Verne write about?

2. Which fish is a 'parr', then a 'smolt' before it swims out to sea?

3. Which 'sailorman' loves spinach?

4. What are coral reefs made of?

5. Which animal gives us pearls? ▶

6. Who was the Roman god of the sea?
   a) Zeus   b) Hercules   c) Neptune

7. What kind of sea creatures are bottle-nosed, Sowerby's, pilot and blue?

8. Which sea separates Britain and Eire?

9. Which fish has to be offered to the Queen if it is caught in British waters?

10. What is the world's largest ocean?

11. What sank the *Titanic*?
    ▶

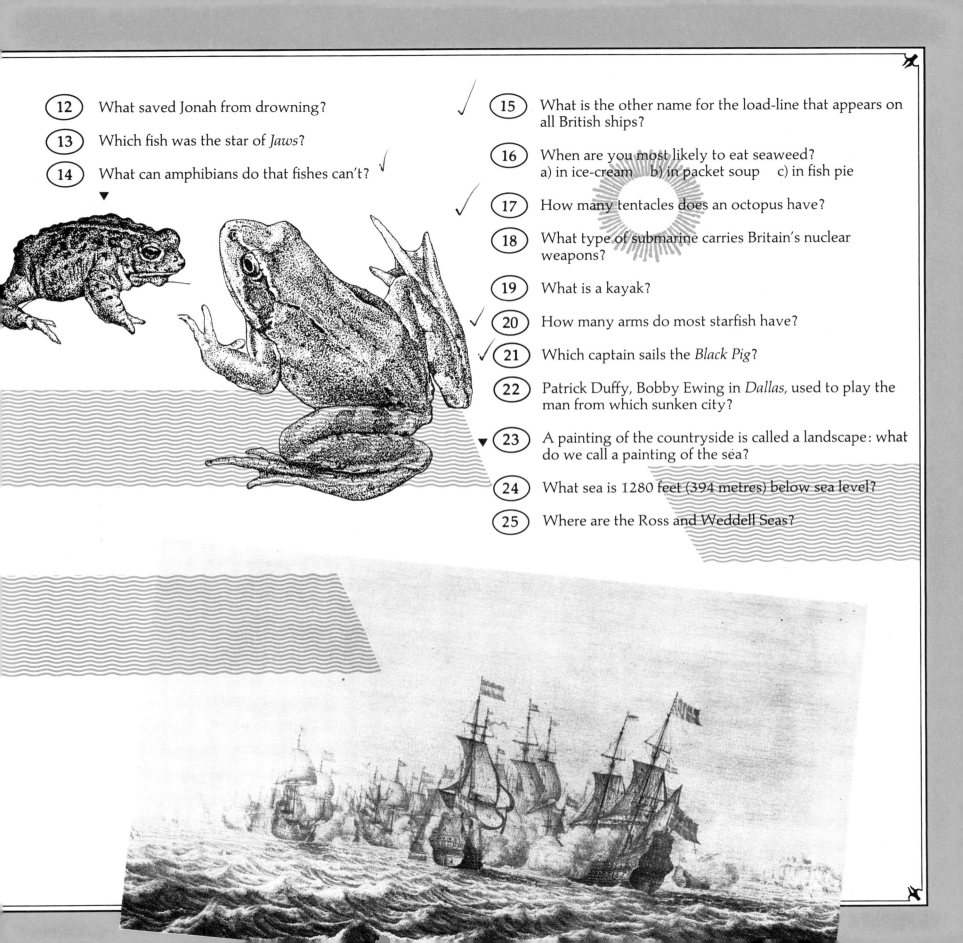

(12) What saved Jonah from drowning?

(13) Which fish was the star of *Jaws*?

(14) What can amphibians do that fishes can't? ▼

(15) What is the other name for the load-line that appears on all British ships?

(16) When are you most likely to eat seaweed?
a) in ice-cream   b) in packet soup   c) in fish pie

(17) How many tentacles does an octopus have?

(18) What type of submarine carries Britain's nuclear weapons?

(19) What is a kayak?

(20) How many arms do most starfish have?

(21) Which captain sails the *Black Pig*?

(22) Patrick Duffy, Bobby Ewing in *Dallas*, used to play the man from which sunken city?

▼ (23) A painting of the countryside is called a landscape: what do we call a painting of the sea?

(24) What sea is 1280 feet (394 metres) below sea level?

(25) Where are the Ross and Weddell Seas?

① In which country did the game Mahjong originate?

② In which game do players knock balls through hoops using mallets?
▼

③ What game was Sir Francis Drake playing when the Armada sailed into view?

④ In which card game do players bid, make contracts and sometimes become dummy?

⑤ What do we call the game known to Americans as checkers?

⑥ In Scrabble, is the bright blue square a triple word, double letter or triple letter?

⑦ How much does it cost to buy a station in Monopoly?

⑧ How many categories are there in Trivial Pursuit?

⑨ When you are playing Charades is it forbidden to speak, move or blink?

⑩ Which chess piece can only move diagonally?
▼

⑪ In which game do players sweep the ice?

⑫ What were Henry Kelly and Jeremy Beadle game for on television?

⑬ How many contenders are there at the start of the Showcase Showdown in *The Price is Right*?

⑭ Which games were revived by Pierre de Coubertin at Athens in 1896?

⑮ In which game do we call 'Legs Eleven!' and 'Key of the Door!'?

19 If you were asked for Miss Bun the Baker's Daughter, what game would you be playing?

20 A card game for one player is called?
a) solitaire   b) patience   c) vingt-et-un

21 When James Bond first came across Goldfinger, what game was the villain playing?

22 What is the plural of dice?
▼

▲
16 √How many pockets are there on a snooker table?

17 At what kind of games would you see someone tossing the caber?

18 What is the maximum you can score with three darts?

23 Which children's rhyme and game reminds us of the Black Death?

√ 24 What game is fair game on the twelfth of August?

25 At which public school would you play the Wall Game?
a) Eton   b) Rugby   c) Harrow

(1) Who did Brutus help to murder?

(2) When did World War I start?

(3) When did the BBC first broadcast television programmes?
a) 1936   b) 1946   c) 1956

(4) Of which country was Tutankhamun king?
▼

(5) What did fletchers make?

(6) What country was ruled by maharajahs?

(7) Who discovered America in 1492?

(8) How many pennies were there in a pound before decimalization?
a) 100   b) 200   c) 240
▼

(9) What destroyed St Paul's Cathedral in 1666?

(10) How many Pope Johns have there been?

(11) Who was king of Albania from 1928–1934?
a) King Zig   b) King Zog   c) King Zag

(12) Which famous French general had a wife called Josephine?

(13) What nationality was William the Conqueror?

(14) Who were the Plantagenets?

(15) What would a Victorian lady have put in a perambulator?

✓ (16) What was Henry VIII's first wife called?

(17) Who was the last Tsar of Russia?
▼

(18) What 'system' did medieval peasants live under?
▼

▲

(19) Where did American colonists have their famous tea party?

(20) Which German monk started the Reformation?

(21) Who did the Roundheads fight against in the English Civil War?

(22) Who had his famous 'last stand' at Little Big Horn?

(23) Which English queen ruled with her husband William III?

✓ (24) Who was the 'Iron Duke'?

(25) What empire had its capital in Vienna?

1. In which London Borough is EastEnders set?
   a) Walford   b) Welford   c) Wellingford

2. Where do Little Bird, Big Bird and the Cookie Monster live?

3. Who fixes it on the BBC?

4. In which street would this character find the Cabin, the Corner Shop and the Café?
   ▼

5. Where are you tickled on ITV?

6. What was the name of Dr Who's metal dog?

7. What is Knight Rider's christian name?

8. What is J.R. Ewing's brother called? ▶ ▶ ▶

▲

9. Which computerised personality hosts a TV chat show?

10. Who had his office in the men's room in Arnold's café?

11. In which city is *The Colbys* set?

12. Which TV hero is a holographic image?

✓ (13) Who calls his wife ''er indoors'?

(14) What television show does Anne Diamond present?

✓ (15) Who says, '. . . This is your Life'?

✓ (16) Who played Dr Who and Worzel Gummidge?

(17) Who hosts *Blankety Blank*?

(18) In which TV series did this actress play a chalet maid? ▶

(19) What is *Blue Thunder*?

(20) What TV series is set in a 'close' in Liverpool?
✓ ▼

(21) Which is the cat, Tom or Jerry? ▶ ▶ ▶ ▶ ▶

(22) Which quiz show for sixth formers does Sue Robbie present?

(23) ✓ What is the longest-running children's TV show?

(24) What TV character did Dr Robert Bruce Banner turn into in times of stress?

(25) Which American sporting event keeps British viewers up well after midnight once a year?

(1) What form of home entertainment was invented by John Logie Baird?

(2) What airplane-tracking device did Sir Robert Watson-Watt invent in 1935?

(3) The man who invented dynamite has a famous prize named after him: who was he?

(4) The first man to fly in the first heavier-than-air machine to fly was
a) Sir George Cayley's coachman   b) Orville Wright
c) Wilbur Wright?

(5) What aid to home cleaning was invented by Mr Bissell in 1876?

(6) Who 'invented' frozen foods?
a) Mr Walls   b) Mr Birdseye   c) Mr Snowie

(7) Who invented the code system based on dots and dashes?
▼

(8) How did the Montgolfier brothers 'fly' in 1783?

(9) Which Ancient Greek scientist and inventor jumped out of the bath shouting 'Eureka'?
▼

(10) Were kites a Japanese, Chinese or Korean invention?
▼

(11) What did the Biro Brothers invent?

(12) Why did the scientists who invented Nylon give it its name?

(13) What was invented at Saratoga Springs in 1853?

(14) Who made the first Kodak camera?
a) George Kodak   b) George Eastman   c) George Ilford

(15) In which English county was Worcestershire Sauce first mixed?

(16) Bonnie Prince Charlie gave the recipe for a famous drink to a Scottish family. Was it
a) Whisky   b) Drambuie   c) beer?

(17) What did Sir Geoffrey de Havilland design?

(18) Which everyday item is said to have been invented by Thomas Crapper?

(19) Who invented the bicycle?
▼

(20) What did Robert Bunsen invent in 1855?

(21) How did an apple help Sir Isaac Newton formulate the ▶ Laws of Gravity?

(22) What cutting device did Leonardo da Vinci invent?

(23) What sea-going invention of David Bushnell might have got him into deep water?

(24) What type of press did Johannes Gutenberg invent?

(25) Did Claus Romer discover the speed of light or the speed of sound in 1675?

(1) In *The Lion, the Witch and the Wardrobe* by C. S. Lewis, how did the children enter the Land of Narnia?

(2) Who shared a cottage with Squirrel and Hare?

(3) What was William's last name?

(4) Where does Paddington's Great-aunt Lucy live?

(5) What is the name of Adrian Mole's girlfriend?

(6) Where did Alice meet Tweedledum and Tweedledee?

(7) What was Biggles' last name?

(8) Who lived in Misselthwaite Manor and found the key to the Secret Garden?

(9) Who married his cousin Celeste and set off for honeymoon in a balloon?

(10) Who went to trap a Heffalump?

(11) What does James Bond have in common with Chitty Chitty Bang Bang?

(12) Who lived and worked at a big station and was looked after by a Fat Controller?

(13) Who was called 'Black Auster', 'Jack', and 'Old Crony' at various times in his life?

(14) If you heard someone claim to be the bravest, most handsome pirate in the Seven Seas, who would you be listening to?

15 Which Nancy solved the mystery of *The Hidden Staircase*?

16 Where did Tom Brown spend his schooldays?

17 What was Captain Hook holding in his right hand when the crocodile bit if off?

18 Who followed a white rabbit down a hole and ended up in Wonderland?

19 Who was Tom Sawyer's best friend?
▼

20 Who wrote *The Little House on the Prairie* books?

21 He wrote a children's book: what was it called?
▼

◄ **22** Who lived in Puddleby-on-the-Marsh and talked to animals?

23 Who said, 'Bloomin' Christmas, here again!'

24 Peter Rabbit and Jeremy Fisher were created by which author?

25 Who goes 'Poop, poop' a lot?

(1) Ena Sharples and Marguerite Hilling are both what, florally speaking?

(2) In what kind of garden would you find Rosemary, Basil and Sweet Cicely?

(3) Do daffodils grow from
a) seeds b) bulbs c) corms?

▼

(4) What disease killed most British elm trees?

(5) One of Britain's great landscape gardeners was?
a) Capability Brown b) Capability Smith
c) Capability Jones.

(6) In which public gardens in London is there a statue of Peter Pan?

▼

(7) Where do plants cultivated in Alpine gardens originate?

(8) Which spring flower is named after a Greek who fell in love with his own reflection?

(9) What kind of gardener grows fruit and vegetables to sell to the public?

(10) What 'garden' in London was famous for its fruit and vegetable market?

▼

(11) What peas are famous climbers and burst into flower?

(12) Golden Wonders and King Edwards are what kind of vegetable?

(13) On what plant do grapes grow? ▶

(14) In which country did chrysanthemums originate?

(15) What colour are the flowers of the runner bean?

(16) Bramleys, Spartans and Golden Delicious are all types of what?

(17) Why do gardeners like ladybirds?

(18) Do hyacinths have a perfume?

(19) Is topiary
a) keeping a lawn in tip-top condition
b) trimming bushes and hedges into artificial shapes
c) bee-keeping?

(20) What colour are dandelion flowers?

(21) What are broad, French and haricot types of?

(22) How long does it take a biennial plant to complete its life cycle?

(23) What part of the eye has the same name as a garden flower?

▼ (24) The heaviest potato grown in Britain weighed
a) 3.1 kg   b) 3.2 kg   c) 3.3 kg?

(25) What flower is named after Leonard Fuchs?

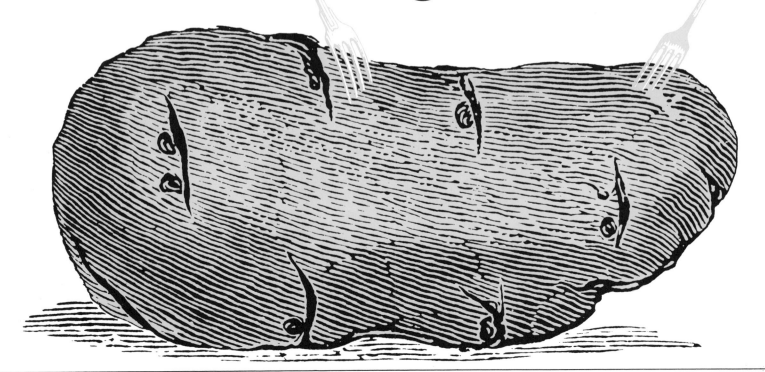

▲

5. How long is the playing time in a netball match?

6. What are the colours of Glasgow Celtic's football strip?

7. In which sport do women compete for the Wightman Cup?

8. On what would you be sitting if you were in a dressage event?

9. Is it allowed to pass the ball forwards in rugby?

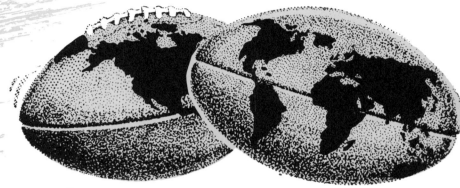

1. How many players are there in Australian Rules football?
   a) 12   b) 15   c) 18

2. In which sport would you hold your breath during a tumble turn?

3. Do golf balls come in varying sizes?   ▶

4. Is a toxopholist an archer, a potholer or a snake collector?

(10) Who competes with the United States for golf's Ryder Cup?

(11) What style of swimming was introduced by Australian Richard Cavill?
a) the backstroke   b) the crawl   c) the doggy paddle

(12) How many test match cricket grounds are there in the UK?

(13) At which race course is the Cheltenham Gold Cup run?

(14) Which Shakespearean character is used to play ice hockey?

(15) In which American sport do players try to make home runs?

(16) What would you be playing if you were going for double top?

(17) What sportsman would use a swim feeder?

(18) Would you be going up or down if you were abseiling?

(19) Which swimming stroke takes its name from a flying insect?

(20) How many people are there on the field when a cricket match is in progress?

(21) What sport do Hull Kingston Rovers play?

(22) What does a snooker referee wear on his hands?

(23) For which sport was American Babe Ruth famous?
a) basketball   b) American football   c) baseball

(24) Which sport was originally called water soccer?

(25) What would you be doing if you were making a roquet?

1. Who said 'Dr Livingstone, I presume'?

2. Which early explorers travelled in long ships and wore helmets with horns?

▼

3. Which king's tomb was opened by Howard Carter and Lord Carnarvon? ▶

4. Who were the Conquistadors?

5. Who discovered Tasmania?
   a) Abel Tasman   b) Jan van Dieman   c) Captain Cook

(6) What nationality was Christopher Columbus?

(7) What was the first ship to sail round the world?

(8) What kind of dogs are used to pull Arctic explorers' sleds?

(9) Who is the patron saint of travellers?

(10) Who was the first man in space? ► ►

(11) What was Sir Francis Drake's ship called?

(12) What nationality was the explorer David Livingstone?
a) Scottish   b) Welsh   c) Irish

▼

(13) What country did Captain Cook discover?

(14) When the Queen knighted round-the-world yachtsman Francis Chichester, whose sword did she use?

(15) Of which country was Henry the Navigator a prince?

(16) In which series of books did Arthur Ransome write about children exploring the Norfolk Broads?

(17) Which 'Scott' was famous for historic explorations?
a) Sir Walter Scott   b) Robert Falcon Scott   c) John Scott

(18) Which father and son explorers sailed from Bristol in the fifteenth and sixteenth centuries?

(19) Which new found land did John Cabot discover?

(20) How many space explorers have walked on Mars?

(21) After which explorer is America named?
a) Amerigo Vespucci   b) Americ the Red   c) America Diaz

(22) Who journeyed across the Antarctic after he had climbed Everest?

(23) What was Robert Peary the first man to reach in 1909?
a) The North Pole   b) The South Pole   c) Timbuctoo

(24) Where did Captain Scott and his men die?

(25) Many explorers went in search of El Dorado. What does *El Dorado* mean?

(1) What sort of animal was Bambi?

(2) Who did Peter Sellers play in *The Pink Panther*?
▼

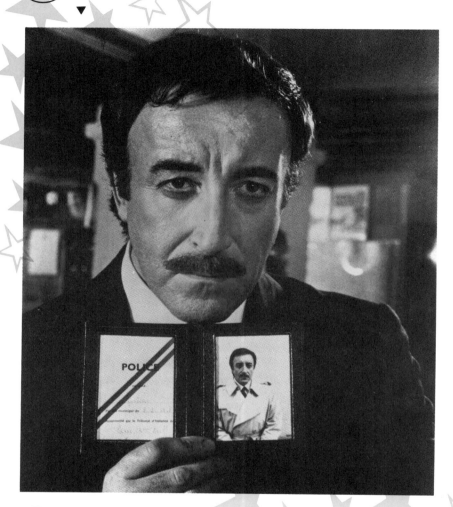

(9) Who is this and what role has he taken over?
▼

(3) How did Jaws II die?

(4) Who went back to the future for his big screen debut? ▶ ▶

(5) Who is the heroine of *The Slipper and the Rose*?

(6) What happens to Pinocchio when he tells a lie?

(7) Who was Professor Pott's girlfriend in *Chitty Chitty Bang Bang*?

(8) What was the middle film in the *Star Wars* trilogy?

(10) What did Mary Poppins do for a living?

(11) Who was Luke Skywalker's father in *Star Wars*?

(12) Which wizard did Richard Pryor play in a 1978 film?

(13) What three numbers is secret agent James Bond known by?

(14) What should you never get wet or feed after midnight?

(15) What were the names of the two robots who starred in *Star Wars*?
▼

(16) What was the name of the mouse detective in one of Walt Disney's recent films?

(17) For which spooky 1984 movie did Ray Parker Junior write the title song? ▶

(18) How many dalmatians are there in the Walt Disney film?

(19) Who straightened the Leaning Tower of Pisa?

(20) Who played the part of Rocky Balboa?

(21) In which movie did Dudley Moore play the part of one of Father Christmas's elves?

(22) What roars at the beginning of every MGM film?

(23) What was the first Muppet Movie called?

(24) What did James Bond tell the tiger to do in *Octopussy*?

(25) What was this character's first name?
▼

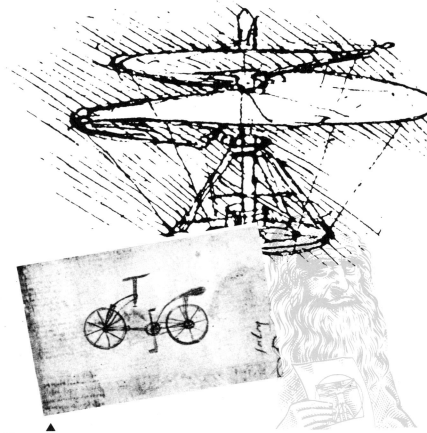

(1) What 'first' did Charles Babbage build in 1827?

(2) Elias Howe patented it in 1846 and Isaac Singer built it some years later. What was it?

(3) Telstar, Echo and Early Bird are all what?

(4) In which industry were the Spinning Jenny and the Flying Shuttle important inventions?
a) textiles   b) printing   c) steelmaking

(5) What kind of machines are VHS and Betamax?

(6) If you were on a Lambretta or a Honda what would you be riding?

(7) What did George Hepplewhite design?
a) furniture   b) bridges   c) firework displays

(8) Where would you tune into MW, LW and FM?

(9) Who designed a flying machine, a primitive bicycle *and* painted *The Last Supper*?

(10) One of Britain's greatest roadbuilders was John Metcalf. Was he deaf, dumb or blind?

(11) What happened to the steam tractor that Nicholas Cugnot built in 1770?
a) It crashed on its first outing   b) It exploded
c) It sank

(12) Was this the first oil well, electric mill or car factory? ▶ ▶

(13) What were *The Rocket* and *The Puffing Billy*?

(14) What art did Joseph Niépce pioneer?
a) Printing   b) Photography   c) Fingerprinting

(15) Is Osmium the heaviest metal, heaviest gas or hardest stone?

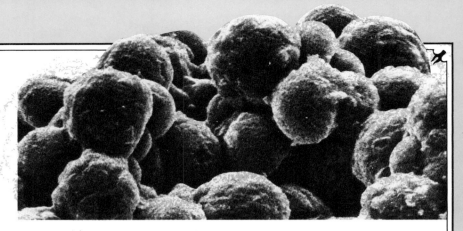

16 Who were the first people to use ivory combs: the Egyptians, the Italians or the Chinese?

17 In which country were sunglasses first worn?
a) France   b) Brazil   c) China

18 What did Anthony van Leeuwenhoek invent that ▶ helped him to discover bacteria?

19 How many eyes are there on a cat's eye on our roads?

20 Are Fiat cars manufactured in Rome, Milan or Turin? ▶

AUTOMOBILES F.I.A.T.

21 What barrier did US Air Force pilot Chuck Yeager first break?

22 In which country were fireworks invented?
a) England   b) China   c) India

23 Which bicycle takes its name from a large coin and a small coin?
▼

24 What is so special about the Harrier jump jet?

25 Was the first parachute jump made in 1797, 1897 or 1927?

7 How did the Pied Piper get his revenge on the councillors of Hamelin? ▶

8 What colour were Bobby Shaftoe's buckles?

9 Where were Uncle Tom Cobbleigh and all going?

10 Which traditional English song mentions parsley, sage, rosemary and thyme?

11 What musical instrument did Sparky play?

12 What burned bright in the forests of the night?

13 Who was scolded for sitting in the cinders?

14 What colours are lavender, Dilly-dilly?

15 What did my darling Clementine's father do for a living?
▶

1 Who looked at his fruity fingers and said 'What a good boy am I'?

2 Who runs through the town in his night gown?

3 What did Little Betty Blue lose?

4 What did my true love send to me on the third day of Christmas?

5 Ding, dong, bell – who is down the well?

6 How many blind mice are there in the nursery rhyme?
▼

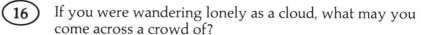

(16) If you were wandering lonely as a cloud, what may you come across a crowd of?

(17) Where does My Bonnie lie?

(18) How many bags of wool did Ba Ba Black sheep have?
▼

(19) Which frog sat halfway down the stairs in a chart song?

(20) How many green bottles hang on the wall to begin with?

(21) What did Marjory Daw do?

(22) Who must have gone away because he wasn't on the stairs?

(23) Is the *Song of Solomon* in the Old or the New Testament?

(24) How many men did the Grand Old Duke of York have in the nursery rhyme?

(25) Who had their tails cut off by the farmer's wife?

1. Which sailor escaped from an island during his second voyage by hitching a lift on a bird?

2. The best ostrich feathers come from male birds. True or false?

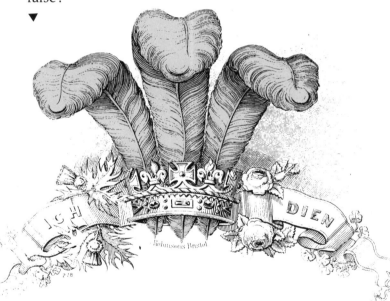

3. What bird is the symbol of the United States?

4. Which pantomime bird lays golden eggs?

5. What's the smallest British bird?

6. What is the most common domestic bird?

7. What's a female peafowl called?

8. Which bird lays its eggs in the nest of others? ▶

9. Which bird has the largest wingspan?

10. What's the collective word for a lot of grouse?

11. Which bird is famous for collecting bright objects?

12. What's a young goose called?

13. A male swan is a cob: what's a female swan?

14 Who killed Cock Robin?

15 Can ostriches fly?
▼

THE TOWER OF LONDON

SEE BR
BY F

▲

16 What birds is the Tower of London famous for?

17 After it leaves its nest, the sooty tern stays in the air for how long before it returns to its breeding grounds?
a) one year   b) two years   c) three years

18 Mallard, eider and mandarin are all types of what?

19 In which sport would you find birdies, eagles and albatrosses?

20 Which bird is also known as the peewit?

◄ **21** Why did the dodo become extinct?

22 What birds do 'fanciers' race?

23 What do we call a man-made bird house?

24 If a bird watcher saw a great-spotted one, what kind of bird would he have seen?

25 The barn, tawny and snowy are all what kind of bird?

1. What do philatelists collect?

2. If you were working with bobbins and threads on a pillow, what would you be making?

3. If your hobby was macramé, what would you do with pieces of string?

4. Sticky hinges are used in what hobby?

5. What knitting stitches are used to form a stocking stitch?

6. Whose favourite weapon is a sword in *Dungeons and Dragons*?

7. Which metal should you not use for fishing weights? ▼

8. Is the boom on a sailing boat horizontal or vertical?

9. What name is used to describe the Japanese art of paper ▶ folding?

10. Which hobby involves 'potting on'?

11. Is orienteering an indoor or outdoor hobby?

12. What would you be doing if you were freefalling?

✓ 13. If you were a speleologist would you be interested in a) spelling   b) weather   c) caves?

14. What does a modern-day angler have in common with a Roman piscator?

15. How old do you have to be before you can legally buy ▶ a pet in England?

16. What kind of cradle is made with string between the hands?

19 What does DIY stand for?

20 If you wanted to take up marquetry would you need wood, feathers or wool?

21 What's an apiarist's hobby?

22 Who are twitchers?

23 What do potters throw?

24 What sort of animal would win the Supreme Championship at Crufts?

25 What does a lepidopterist collect?
a) butterflies   b) newspapers   c) watches
▼

17 If you bred Black Hollies, Wagtails and Cape Lopez Lyretails what would your hobby be?

18 What do you call people who collect coins?
a) numismatologists   b) metallurgists
c) campanologists
▼

Pickings by a Newfoundland Doggie!

LICENCE

1. What is the capital of Algeria?

2. What is the largest desert in Africa?

3. Do tigers live wild in Africa?

4. What's the shortest distance between Africa and Europe?
   a) 14 km   b) 140 km   c) 1400 km

5. Which country's system of *Apartheid* has made it unpopular with other nations?

6. When Zaire was Congo, was it the personal property of
   a) Queen Victoria   b) King Leopold of the Belgians
   c) King Philip of Spain

7. What is Africa's longest river?

8. Which African canal was opened in 1869 and links the Red Sea with the Mediterranean?

9. Which African country benefited from Live Aid, Band Aid and Sports Aid?

10. If you were in Nairobi with a pocketful of shillings, in which country would you be?

11. To which European country did Algeria once belong?

12. What large island lies off the south-east coast of Africa?

13. Which ocean lies off the west coast of Africa?

14. As what kind of continent was Africa once described?

15. Is the Sahara Desert north or south of the Equator?

16. Which Swahili word means 'to hunt' and 'journey'?

17. Mumbo Jumbo is
    a) an African elephant   b) an African god
    c) an African river?

18. Which bird is the only one that produces leather?

19. Which African desert do the bushmen of the Kalahari call home?

20. What is this ancient Egyptian monument called?

▼

21. What did Rhodesia change its name to?

22. Which African athlete changed her nationality so that she could run in the 1984 Olympics?

23. Which African animal is hunted for its ivory?

24. In which African country do Zulus live?

25. What are the smallest people of Africa known as?

(1) What sort of animal is Biffo?

(2) What did pantomime Jack swap for his mother's cow?

(3) Whose dog is Jumble?
a) William Brown's   b) The Secret Seven's   c) Milly-Molly-Mandy's

(4) Who was Brer Rabbit's enemy?

(5) Who wrote *The Jungle Book*?
▼

(6) What does Alice chase down the rabbit hole in *Alice in Wonderland*?

(7) What kind of animals lived in *Watership Down*?

(8) Who steals the sausages in a Punch and Judy show?

(9) Which cat loves pizza but hates spinach?
▼

(10) Is Lassie a German Shepherd dog, a Labrador or a Collie?
▼

11. In *Animal Farm* what kind of animal was Napoleon?

12. What monstrous animal lives in a Scottish loch?

13. What kind of animal is Rupert?

14. In *The Jungle Book* is Shere Khan a tiger, a leopard or a lion?

15. What kind of cat does Alice come across in her travels?

16. Do the Queen's dogs eat tinned dog food?
▼

▲

19. Which London landmark is guarded by four statues of this animal?

20. What kind of animal was Elsa, written about in *Born Free*?

21. Who rode a horse called Black Bess?

22. Who did the spider ask into its parlour?

23. Is Rin Tin Tin a dog, a cat or a rat?

24. According to Aesop, which animal beat the hare in a race?

25. What kind of animal was the Darling children's nanny in *Peter Pan*?

17. Which Scottish dog remained faithfully by his master's ▶ grave for many years?

18. Which famous comic was named after a bird?
a) *The Eagle*   b) *The Buzzard*   c) *The Falcon*

THE ANSWERS

1 · PP · Countries and Capitals

1 The Statue of Liberty. It was a gift to the USA from the people of France and was erected in 1886
2 The River Thames in London
3 In Edinburgh, the capital of Scotland. The Castle overlooks Princes' Street Gardens
4 Monaco, the tiny principality situated between France and Italy
5 Paris, the capital of France
6 Rome. He is said to have played a musical instrument while the city burned down in AD64
7 In Copenhagen, capital of Denmark. She is called *The Little Mermaid*
8 Switzerland and Italy. The Great St Bernard Pass is 53 miles (85 kilometres) long. The Little St Bernard Pass is 39 miles (63 kilometres long)
9 Peking, the capital of China
10 The Argentinians, who claim them as their territory
11 The Black Sea. Romania, USSR, Turkey and Bulgaria also have Black Sea coastlines
12 On the other side of the world. It's the name we give to Australia and New Zealand
13 Hispaniola in the Caribbean Sea
14 In Australia, near Sydney
15 Israel. It is the official language of the country
16 c) Aberdeen. Many of the buildings there are built of locally-quarried granite
17 In Spain. It's a dish made from rice, shellfish, chicken and vegetables
18 In Venice, Italy. The city is famous for its canals
19 Paris. Leonardo da Vinci's famous painting *The Mona Lisa* hangs in the Louvre Gallery
20 Verona, their home town in the play by William Shakespeare
21 In Scotland. It's called Tossing the Caber
22 In Denver, where the soap opera *Dynasty* is set
23 At sea. The Doldrums is an area of ocean near the Equator where there is little wind and very calm seas
24 In Eire, not far from Cork. Kissing the Blarney Stone is said to make you very eloquent
25 In Turkey. The Ark came to rest on Mount Ararat

2 · GT · Chart Toppers

1 Curiosity Killed the Cat
2 Pet Shop Boys
3 a) Grammies
4 Sting
5 He fell to earth. David Bowie starred in *The Man Who Fell to Earth*
6 The Bangles
7 c) Paul McCartney
8 The Communards
9 Paul Simon
10 b) Blue Turtle Blues
11 Blancmange
12 John (Lennon), Paul (McCartney), George (Harrison) and Ringo (Starr)
13 Genesis
14 'The King'. As you can see from the picture it's Elvis Presley
15 Billy Idol
16 Lionel Richie
17 Pink Floyd
18 Duran Duran
19 'Dancing in the Street'
20 Spandau Ballet
21 'Let It Be'
22 The Who
23 Freddie Mercury
24 Siouxsie
25 Five Star

3 · ST · The Human Body

1 *Gluteus Maximus* (the muscle in the buttocks). The illustration is the statue of David, by Michelangelo
2 32. 16 in the top and 16 in the bottom jaw
3 It's a gland – the largest in the human body
4 The tongue. Every other muscle is attached to another part of the body at both ends
5 The one on the middle finger
6 37°C (98.6°F). The highest human temperature ever recorded is 46.5°C (115.7°F) in 1980
7 The heart. They are the chambers of that organ
8 Your eyes. Your eyes close automatically when you sneeze
9 He was the tallest man ever measured – 8ft 11.1 in (2.72 metres)
10 Tooth and gum decay. We all suffer from it at some point
11 c) 2 500 000. Pores are tiny 'holes' in the skin through which we perspire
12 A man. On average it is 9oz (215g) heavier than a woman's
13 c) B1 in 1910
14 Pollen. It makes sufferers from hay fever sneeze and their eyes water
15 Carbon Dioxide
16 b) 2/3
17 b) 206 (although the number can vary by one or two)
18 In the ear. The stirrup bone measures 0.17in (3.4mm) at most
19 Intelligence Quotient – the way we measure how intelligent we are
20 The appendix. The illustration shows the demonstration theatre in Padua, Italy, where surgeons showed students how to perform operations from the 17th century
21 In the eye
22 Blood
23 c) smell
24 Blood groups
25 b) 4.5 litres – 8 pints

4 · AC · Costume

1 On the shoulders of a military uniform: the word comes from the French *epaule* which means shoulder
2 Vicars and other clergymen
3 Bell bottoms, because they have very wide bottoms, originally made to enable sailors to roll them up when scrubbing the decks
4 Panama, where the famous canal is
5 A woman. It's a padded roll worn under the skirt to expand it
6 a) a skirt: it's part of the national costume of southern Germany and Austria
7 A hat named after the heroine of a novel by George du Maurier
8 a) Arthur Wellesley, first Duke of Wellington. He was a soldier during the Napoleonic Wars and later Prime Minister of Britain
9 Charles Macintosh. He took out a patent for it in 1823
10 a) a deerstalker. Sherlock Holmes was created by Arthur Conan Doyle who is shown with Holmes in the picture
11 Leather. They are the shorts widely worn by men in Austria and Germany
12 c) Lacoste. The company makes sports clothes
13 David and Elizabeth Emanuel. Copies of the dress were in some shops a few hours after the wedding!
14 A female ballet dancer. It's a short skirt made of layers of stiff material
15 Silks
16 Usually wood
17 Greece. The skirt is part of the ceremonial uniform worn by soldiers who guard public buildings in Athens
18 A spray of flowers pinned to the bodice of a dress
19 Stilettos. The heels of these shoes are very high and pointed
20 A yashmak. Today only strict followers of the Islamic faith wear the veil
21 Bermuda shorts, first worn by the islanders on Bermuda. Policemen on the island still wear them as part of their uniform
22 b) It was first made in Nimes. The cloth *de Nimes* became known as denim
23 Down his right sock. It's a small ceremonial dagger with a semi-precious stone set in the handle
24 A woman who is expecting a baby
25 The Sari. It's a long piece of silk or cotton wrapped around the body

5 · NW · Farmyard Facts

1 c) 4 500 000 000
2 George Orwell (1903–1950). He wrote many famous books including *1984* and *The Road to Wigan Pier*
3 Pigs. Despite the expression 'living in a pig sty', pigs are very clean animals
4 They are all types of cattle
5 Fish farms. The fish eggs are hatched in hatcheries and when the fish are large enough they are put into large ponds where they are fattened up
6 Collies – usually bearded and border collies
7 A billy goat. Female goats are called nanny goats and young goats are kids
8 Pigs. The disease is very infectious
9 Crops. The farmer is resting the soil for a growing season before replanting with crops
10 Rice. Paddy fields are kept under a shallow layer of water
11 Doves
12 a) 'Turnip' Townsend (1674–1738). He encouraged his tenants to grow turnips, hence his nickname
13 Green
14 Cattle. The correct expression is 'ruminating'
15 a) barley. Cabbage is a vegetable crop and cotton an industrial one
16 Chemicals. They believe that artificial fertilisers can damage crops
17 Farmyard birds, such as chickens, turkeys and geese
18 Silage – fodder crops that are harvested while green and stored as feed for farm animals
19 The Minister of Agriculture, Fisheries and Food
20 A goatherd
21 Sunnybrook Farm, in the novels by Kate Douglas Wiggin. The illustration shows Shirley Temple in the film
22 Cattle. A byre is a cowshed
23 Chickens
24 c) George III (1738–1820), because of his keen interest in agriculture
25 One that is given over to crop-rearing rather than animals

6 · GH · Ball Sports

1 Rugby Football. The Irish play at Landsowne Park and the Scots at Murrayfield
2 Three. A red one and two white ones, one with a dot on it
3 Ten. Four in the back line, three in front of them, two in front of them and one at the very front
4 b) Berkshire
5 Centre Court – the one where the finals are played
6 Ten. The game was originally played by North American Indians
7 The Arsenal. Its nickname is 'The Gunners'
8 The pink. Reds score one each, yellow two, green three, brown four, blue five and black seven
9 Czechoslovakia. Lendl and Navratilova are now based in USA. Mandlikova is married to an Australian
10 Eighteen. On a score card the first nine holes are 'out' and the second nine 'in'
11 You are not allowed to bounce the ball, unless you are passing it to another player
12 Pool. The film was a sequel to *The Hustler* which starred Paul Newman who was also in *The Color of Money*
13 They are added to your opponent's score
14 The LTA allow yellow balls to be used at some tournaments
15 Yes. Cardiff City beat Arsenal 1–0 in the 1927 Cup Final
16 New York
17 Marylebone Cricket Club. Its headquarters are at Lords in London
18 Golf. The Royal and Ancient at St Andrews is the game's ultimate world authority
19 A shuttlecock. A circle of feathers embedded in a cork base
20 Yes. The pitch in Canadian Football is larger and there is one more player in each team. There are also some minor differences in the rules
21 Bowls. Players try to roll their bowls as close as they can to a small white ball called the 'Jack'
22 Five. The Men's and Ladies' Singles; the Men's and Ladies' Doubles and the Mixed Doubles
23 b) chukkas. There are eight, seven-minute chukkas in each game
24 Seven. Football, Basketball, Handball, Hockey, Volleyball, Tennis and Water Polo
25 Ireland. It's a ball game played with sticks between two teams of fifteen players each

7 · PP · Famous Names

1 The Pope. St Peter was the first Bishop of Rome
2 Salome. Her step-father was King Herod
3 Nancy. She's Mrs Ronald Reagan
4 Marie Antoinette (1755–1793), wife of Louis XVI. She was executed a few months after her husband
5 Sir Winston Churchill (1874–1965). He was defeated in the General election of 1945 by Clement Attlee
6 Margaret Thatcher, Britain's first woman prime minister
7 George O'Dowd. He's better known as Boy George
8 Judas Iscariot – for thirty pieces of silver
9 Florence Nightingale (1820–1910)
10 Julius Caesar. It means, 'I came, I saw, I conquered'
11 Peter Phillips, son of Princess Anne (the Princess Royal) and Captain Mark Phillips. He was born in 1977
12 Louis Bleriot – on July 15, 1909
13 Mozart's. He was born in 1756 and died in 1791
14 Queen Victoria. Victoria was her second name and she chose to be known by it when she came to the throne in 1837. She died in 1901
15 Sir Christopher Wren (1632–1723)
16 Mary, Queen of Scots. She inherited the Scottish throne in 1542 when she was a week old. Her first husband was King of France for a short time, and she believed, as a Roman Catholic, that she was the true Queen of England. She was executed in 1587
17 John Craven
18 The Princess of Wales. Mrs Cartland's daughter is the Princess's step-mother
19 George Washington (1732–1799)
20 Elizabeth I (1533–1603). She was the daughter of Henry VIII and Anne Boleyn
21 William Shakespeare (1564–1616), the great playwright
22 John F. Kennedy. He was only 43 when he was elected in 1960. He was assassinated in Dallas, Texas, in 1963
23 Neil Armstrong on July 20, 1969
24 Field-Marshal Montgomery (1887–1976)
25 Sarah Ferguson. Prince Andrew was created Duke of York on the morning of their wedding in 1986

8 · GT · Pop's the Question

1 A-Ha, from Norway
2 George Michael and Andrew Ridgeley
3 Michael Caine
4 Paul Young. It was the title of his hit album that year
5 The Communards
6 Five
7 UB40
8 *The Phantom of the Opera*, by Andrew Lloyd Webber
9 Madonna
10 The E Street Band
11 Tina Turner
12 Genesis
13 A werewolf and then a zombie
14 Daryl Hall and John Oates
15 Hollywood. The group is Frankie Goes to Hollywood
16 There were three of them
17 Anita Dobson (Angie) and Nick Berry (Wicksy)
18 Yazoo
19 Bob Geldof, but because he is an Irish citizen he cannot call himself Sir Bob
20 Nick Kamen, who featured in the Levis 501 commercial
21 U2
22 'Do They Know It's Christmas?'. It sold around 40 million copies in aid of the Ethiopian Famine Relief Appeal
23 ABBA is the initials of the first names of the group – Agnetha, Bjorn, Benny and Anni-Frid
24 Dave Stewart
25 Pet Shop Boys

9 · ST · All Shapes and Sizes

1 Yes. A square is a rectangle with four equal sides
2 c) three equal sides
3 360
4 Six
5 Sphere
6 Geometry
7 60° – the angles of a triangle add up to 180°
8 Because the building has five sides – a pentagon
9 A cubic metre
10 Three
11 Six
12 The Oval, at Kennington in London
13 A boxing ring
14 Round. They were called Roundheads because of their short haircuts
15 Eight
16 Squares
17 Cones
18 SHAPE
19 Pyramids. We can still see them in Egypt
20 Square
21 On a cricket field: it's one of the fielding positions
22 A straight line
23 Albert Square
24 Toblerone
25 The Bermuda Triangle

10 · AC · Religions and Traditions

1 When he is thirteen. On the first sabbath after his thirteenth birthday full membership of the Jewish faith is conferred on him at a *Bar Mitzvah* Ceremony
2 Thanksgiving Day. It commemorates the gathering of the first harvest
3 Good Friday – the Friday before Easter Sunday
4 Confucianism – the main religion in China
5 a) Islam. *Ayatollahs* are the holy men of the Shi'ite Muslims
6 Twelve. Andrew, Peter, James, John, Philip, Bartholomew, Thomas, Matthew, James (son of Alphaeus), Jude, Simon and Judas
7 The May Day Parade, when Soviet troops parade in front of members of the *Politburo*
8 Islam. Mohammed was born there and it was to the city that he returned after his famous Flight From Mecca of 622 when he took refuge in Medina
9 The five ks. The kesh is long, uncut hair. The kangha, a comb. The katcha are knee-length shorts. The kara is a bracelet. And the kirpan a sword
10 Hallowe'en – October 31
11 Saturday. It officially begins when the first three stars appear in the sky on Friday night and lasts for 24 hours
12 Lamb
13 Prince Albert, Queen Victoria's husband
14 An elephant's head. The God is called Ganesk
15 Roman Catholics. The Society was founded by Ignatius Loyola in 1534
16 c) First footing
17 Gold, Frankincense and Myrrh
18 Mistletoe
19 Forty days, from Ash Wednesday to Holy Saturday
20 On April 23 (which is also, by tradition, Shakespeare's birthday)
21 Because there is a tradition that there is a vein or nerve running from that finger to the heart. There isn't in fact
22 Holly ones decorated with red ribbons
23 Two. Her real birthday on April 21 and her official one on the second Saturday in June when one of her Guards' regiments troops their colours before her on Horseguards' Parade in London
24 Laurel crowns
25 The Queen. The title was awarded to Henry VIII by Pope Leo X in 1521

11 · NW · Four Legs

1 The cheetah. Over short distances it can reach 70mph (112km/h)
2 The camel, which can last for long periods without drinking.
3 The Grand National, which is run at Aintree in Liverpool
4 The fox
5 The rat. During the Black Death more than 25 million Europeans died
6 Grey
7 The giant panda, which lives wild only in parts of China
8 Probably the dog
9 The sloth. Some sloths appear to change colour because of an algae that grows in their fur!
10 The jerboa
11 The mammoth
12 Yes. They are very shy creatures usually only seen at night
13 Beavers. Some of the dams are so large, they change the course of rivers
14 Fish
15 The Saint Bernard. The dogs are often used as rescue dogs in the Alps
16 The elephant. They can weigh up to 12.24 tonnes
17 Five
18 Four. The rumen, the reticulum, the manyplies and the abdomen
19 To hear with
20 c) A hare. It can reach 45 mph (72 km/h)
21 The cat
22 A mouse, in his poem *To a Mouse*
23 An elk
24 The ermine. Ermine fur is very highly prized by some people
25 A pride

12 · GH · Track and Field

1 Dr Roger Bannister. He ran it in 3 minutes, 59.4 seconds in 1954
2 Four
3 26 miles . . . and 385 yards. The odd number of yards is because Queen Alexandra wanted to be seated opposite the finishing line when the Olympics were held in London in 1908. Rather than move the Royal Box the organisers added 385 yards onto the marathon distance
4 Steve Cram and Sebastian Coe
5 a) 16 lbs (7.257 kg)
6 Five – riding, fencing, shooting, swimming and cross-country running
7 South African
8 Dick Fosbury
9 Daley Thompson. He won the Olympic gold medal in 1980 and 1984
10 b) 1000 kilometres
11 The 50 kilometre walk
12 Javelin throwing
13 Amateur Athletics Association
14 Eight
15 Eight – hammer, discus, shot-putting, high and long jump, pole vault, javelin and triple jump
16 Six
17 The five continents of the world
18 No. The throw counts as long as the javelin lands tip first
19 The hammer
20 At Stoke Mandeville in 1948. The hospital there is famous for treating disabled people
21 The triple jump
22 100 metres
23 No
24 Fifteen miles an hour
25 a) in 776 BC

13 · PP · The Orient

1 Japan's
2 Marco Polo. It took him four years to get there!
3 Peking (which is now called Beijing)
4 Portugal. It consists of a small peninsula and two tiny islands
5 The Great Wall of China
6 Mount Fuji – 12 398 feet (3780 metres) high
7 Hong Kong
8 a) a Japanese robe
9 The willow. Willow pattern plates originally came from Japan
10 *The King and I*. The illustration shows Yul Brynner as The King and Deborah Kerr as the Governess, Anna
11 b) The Sea of Japan
12 In China
13 Up the sleeves of their robes. It's a Pekingese
14 South Vietnam (now part of Vietnam)
15 c) Japan. The sport is Sumo Wrestling
16 The Philippines. He now lives in exile in Hawaii
17 The yen.
18 b) fish
19 *The Mikado*
20 The Tropic of Cancer
21 Silk. They are silk worms
22 b) No. No Theatre is very stylized classical drama that uses music, dancing and themes from religious stories. It dates from the fifteenth century
23 Victoria
24 The art of growing miniature trees
25 Shanghai

14 · GT · Stars of the Screen

1. a) River Phoenix
2. Michael Jackson. He signed an agreement with Pepsi in 1986 to endorse the drink for a reputed $50 000 000
3. John Lennon. He was shot outside his apartment near Central Park
4. Robert Redford. He starred in *Butch Cassidy and the Sundance Kid* with Paul Newman and in *Out of Africa* with Meryl Streep
5. Roland Rat
6. Prince
7. Cliff Richard. He sang 'Bachelor Boy' in *Summer Holiday* and starred in the stage musical *Time* in London
8. a) Barbra
9. John MacEnroe and Tatum O'Neal
10. b) The Bratpack
11. Joseph
12. Ronnie Corbett. He starred in the TV series *Sorry!*
13. Sean Penn
14. b) The Goons
15. c) Emma Samms who plays Fallon in *Dynasty* and *The Colbys*
16. Mel Gibson
17. David Bowie
18. Christopher Reeve
19. He was a carpenter
20. Ronald Reagan
21. Dame Edna Everage
22. Michael
23. Woody Allen
24. Tom Cruise
25. Elvis Presley's widow Priscilla. She plays Jenna

15 · ST · On Wheels

1. A BMX
2. With your foot
3. A red flag. The 1865 Red Flag Act imposed a speed limit of 4 mph (6.5 km/h) in the country and half that in towns and required that a man carrying a red flag walk in front of cars. It was not repealed until 1896
4. Harley Davidson
5. The chain
6. A skateboard
7. Red
8. Rolls Royce
9. Neutral
10. Two – and two saddles
11. a) 1832 when a stoker on a steam omnibus was killed when it exploded
12. Hitler. He wanted a car for all the people, hence *Volks* (people's) *wagen* (car)
13. A Ministry of Transport Certificate of Roadworthiness. All cars over three years old have to have one
14. c) 1190 km/h, held by Stan Barrett in his rocket-powered *Budweiser Rocket* at Edwards Air Base in 1979
15. Datsun, a Japanese company
16. London and Venice. The train sets off from Victoria Station in London
17. *Starlight Express*
18. Motor cycle racing
19. b) black
20. A De Lorean
21. A track where cycle races are held
22. Through the window
23. The M1
24. Alternately at Brands Hatch and Silverstone
25. Postman Pat

16 · AC · Traditions and Sayings

1. Sheep's clothing
2. Nine
3. One swallow doth not a summer make
4. Magpies
5. You would be travelling on foot
6. Too many cooks spoil the broth
7. Stones
8. Envy
9. The hatchet
10. The early bird catches the worm
11. Dead men don't tell tales
12. Your ears
13. Bugs Bunny
14. Marry in haste, repent at leisure
15. Poor. The expression is 'As poor as a church mouse'
16. A new broom sweeps clean
17. The rain in Spain falls mainly on the plain
18. 'Turn again Whittington, thrice mayor of London'
19. Two heads are better than one
20. All that glitters is not gold
21. Good weather. Red sky at night is the shepherd's delight
22. You may as well be hung for a sheep than a lamb
23. It's out of mind
24. On the other side of the hill
25. A bird in the hand is worth two in the bush

17 · NW · Natural Wonders

1. Volcanoes. They are both in Italy
2. San Francisco. Some geologists believe that another major earthquake could threaten California at any time
3. b) it appeared off the coast of Iceland
4. Lava
5. The Great Barrier Reef
6. New Zealand. Maoris call one of the regions of that country *Takiwa-Waiarike* – the land of hot water
7. The Niagara Falls
8. b) the Colorado
9. The Dead Sea. It is so salty that swimmers float easily
10. A mirage
11. Norway. Fjords are large sea inlets
12. Mount Everest. It is 29 028 feet (8 848 metres) high
13. a) about one eighth
14. The Caspian Sea – 139 000 miles² (360 700 km²)
15. Discounting Australia, which is a continent, it's Greenland with an area of 840 000 miles² (2 175 000 km²)
16. Yes. Two men were killed as a result of an earthquake that shook London in 1580
17. A rainbow
18. No. But it did reach 98.2°F in 1911 in some places in the south of England
19. Hurricanes
20. Huge tidal waves may form
21. The Himalayas
22. The Victoria Falls
23. White
24. b) The Severn. It's 220 miles (354 km) long
25. a) 11 700 years old. It's a *Larrea tridentata* in California

18 · GH · Records and Champions

1. John Curry at the 1976 Winter Olympics at Montreal
2. Cliff Thorburn
3. b) 7. Four individual ones and three team ones
4. A white shark. It weighed 2 664 lbs (1 208 kg) and was caught in 1959
5. Chess. He was only 22 when he won the title in 1985
6. He scored 36 runs (six sixes) off one over
7. The long jump – at 29 ft 2.5 in (8.90 metres)
8. c) horse racing. He is an American jockey
9. Gentleman Jim Corbett. He defeated John Sullivan for the title in 1892 after 21 rounds
10. Martina Navratilova
11. The Equestrian Three-day Event. She won the title in 1971
12. a) 886, struck by Allie Brandt of New York in 1939
13. Horse racing
14. Torvill and Dean. At the World Ice Dance Championships in 1984 they were awarded 29 '6s'
15. b) Jack Nicklaus. He won his sixth US Masters title in 1986
16. Scottish
17. Ian Botham, the one in the foreground. The other is David Gower
18. Juan Fangio. He won in 1951, 1954, 1955, 1956, and 1957
19. England, France, Ireland, Scotland and Wales
20. a) £1 032 088 in April, 1987
21. a) Jack Hobbs. He made 197 centuries in 1315 innings
22. Boxing. They were both world heavyweight champions
23. Speed skating. He holds the world 500 metres title in 45.08 secs
24. Right-handed
25. a) It is 467.5 kg (1030.5 lbs) by Russian Leonid Taranenko in 1986

19 · PP · The Americas

1 The Panama Canal
2 San Francisco in California
3 Five – Superior, Huron, Michigan, Erie and Ontario
4 The Andes
5 Havana
6 Bolivia. Bolivar liberated much of South America from European rule
7 The jaguar
8 On Sundays
9 Spanish. A great part of South America was once ruled by Spain
10 Fifty – one for each state
11 Alaska, off north-west Canada, and Hawaii, in the Pacific
12 California. It's the centre of the movie industry
13 b) Victoria
14 The Amazon. It's 4080 miles (6570 kilometres) long
15 Mexico. The Spanish overthrew them in the sixteenth century
16 Jamaica
17 Totem Poles
18 Mounties
19 La Paz. It is 11 916 feet (3 361 metres) above sea level
20 Mexico
21 It is a bird. The Californian condor is the largest bird of prey in the world
22 Chile
23 a) 65 km – the narrowest point of the Bering Strait that separates them
24 The llama
25 American universities

20 · GT · Comics and Cartoons

1 He's the idiot in the *Topper*
2 Colonel Blink
3 Oor Wullie
4 A dog. (A Basset hound)
5 Garfield
6 The *Dandy*
7 Big Bird
8 Sid's snake in *Whizzer*
9 Desperate Dan and Desperate Dog
10 Superman
11 Spiderman
12 Robin
13 A top hat
14 Snoopy
15 Tricky Dicky
16 A gerbil
17 Snowy
18 Miss Piggy
19 Flash Gordon's
20 Bully Beef
21 Toytown
22 Madame Cholet
23 Blue
24 The Sorceror in the Walt Disney film *Fantasia*. It's Mickey Mouse
25 Sunnysides

21 · ST · Simple Science

1 An acid
2 Because it helps keep the heat inside the building
3 So they won't get electric shocks
4 a) H
5 It boils
6 Light waves. They travel at 186 281 mps (299 793 km/s)
7 Seven. Violet, Indigo, Blue, Green, Yellow, Orange and Red
8 North. (To be accurate, it points to magnetic north)
9 a) direct current
10 No. Many lenses are now made of plastic
11 The skull
12 It curves outwards. A concave surface curves inwards
13 Oil
14 a) uranium
15 Honey
16 Laser beams
17 At the top
18 They hope it will rain
19 Computers. Hardware is the actual machines. Softwear is the programmes that are used in the system
20 b) sulphuric
21 Microwaves
22 Because it is sulphuric acid!
23 Green and yellow. The other two wires are blue and brown
24 c) nothing
25 a) oil

22 · AC · Music Making

1 The piano
2 ABBA. One of their hits was 'Thank You for the Music.'
3 Four – two violinists, a cellist and one who plays the viola
4 a) a celesta. A celesta is a small keyboard instrument
5 Arthur Sullivan wrote the music
6 A piano. The piece was named when a German poet said it reminded him of moonlight on the sea
7 Mozart. He also wrote *The Magic Flute, The Marriage of Figaro*, and many other operas
8 Antonio Stradivari (1644–1737). He also made cellos
9 A band has no stringed instruments in it
10 *Pianoforte*. It was invented by a Florentine called Cristofino in 1709
11 A tenor
12 Ringo Starr. A tympanist is a drummer
13 He wrote *Rhapsody in Blue*
14 c) Ravel's *Bolero*
15 The Spanish guitar
16 The flute. He has a solid gold one
17 Compact disc
18 St Cecilia. According to tradition, she invented the organ
19 The dead
20 Beethoven. He wrote nine altogether
21 b) the double bass
22 He is best known for his waltzes. He also wrote polkas and gallops
23 Australia. It is an aborigine instrument
24 Alan A'Dale. He played the lute
25 The organ

23 · NW · Plant Life

1 They store it in their stems
2 A West Indian vegetable also known as a 'sweet potato'
3 Bananas
4 Green
5 It's a fruit
6 A dried plum
7 Yes
8 The vine. It's distilled from grape wine
9 They grow below ground
10 Oak trees
11 It's dead
12 It's a dried grape
13 It's tapped from the bark of a tree called *Hevea brasiliensis*
14 Avocado pear
15 They are types of lettuce
16 In a flower. A sepal is any of the separate parts of the calyx
17 a) heliotropism
18 The Busy Lizzie
19 a) The gas plant
20 Mushrooms (but don't try to pick them yourself: some fungi look like mushrooms, but are very poisonous)
21 a) The Biggest Aspidistra in the World
22 The leaves. During photosynthesis the green chlorophyl in the leaves converts the sun's energy into food and oxygen is given off as a by-product
23 They are all ferns
24 The blackberry (in some parts of Britain it is called the bramble)
25 The stamen

24 · GH · Clubs and Societies

1 The Boy's Brigade
2 Cruelty to children. It is the National Society for the Prevention of Cruelty to Children
3 At Richmond
4 Accidents. It is the Royal Society for the Prevention of Accidents
5 Culture Club
6 a) The Women's Institute
7 Royal Society for the Prevention of Cruelty to Animals
8 HRH the Princess Margaret, Countess of Snowdon
9 c) The House of Lords
10 Young Men's Christian Association
11 b) films. It's the National Film Theatre
12 At London Zoo, in Regent's Park
13 Bird watching. The RSPB is the Royal Society for the Protection of Birds
14 The Boy Scouts
15 a) The Young Farmers
16 The Brownies
17 Wolf Cubs
18 The Boy Scouts
19 Members of St John Ambulance Brigade
20 c) theatre. It is the Royal Shakespeare Company
21 Jesuits. The Society was founded by Ignatius Loyola in 1534
22 The Outlaws, in the William books by Richmal Crompton
23 Motorists. They are the Automobile Association and Royal Automobile Club
24 b) at Wimbledon in London
25 a) The Royal Society

25 · PP · Down Under

1 Canberra, midway between Melbourne and Sydney
2 A penal settlement for convicted convicts
3 *Endeavour*
4 A marsupial. Their young are born before they are completely developed and continue to grow in a pouch on their mother's belly
5 Aborigines
6 Tasmania
7 North Island and South Island
8 The kiwi
9 The All Blacks
10 Sydney
11 Northern Territory. The others are Queensland, New South Wales, Victoria, South Australia and Western Australia
12 Edinburgh
13 Paul Hogan
14 Ned Kelly. He was hanged in Melbourne in 1880
15 Ayers Rock in the Northern Territory
16 Dingoes. They were introduced into Australia from Ceylon or Malaya
17 Sir Edmund Hillary
18 The Indian Ocean
19 An emu
20 Maoris
21 The Murray-Darling (2230 miles – 3750 kilometres – long)
22 Mount Cook – 12 346 feet (3750 metres) high
23 Koala bears
24 Sheep. These countries are the world's leading producers of wool
25 b) 1930 miles

26 · GT · News and Views

1 No. When Britain decided to join in 1972, the Norwegians held a referendum the result of which was to stay out. Britain joined on January 1, 1973
2 In the Lebanon where a civil war has been raging for many years
3 a) Fidel Castro. His troops forced President Batista to flee in 1959. Castro has been president ever since
4 The Republicans and the Democrats
5 a) Strategic Arms Limitation Talks
6 The Alliance
7 Polish. He was born Karol Wojtyla in 1920. He is the first non-Italian pope since 1552
8 No. They can be ordained as deacons and carry out some pastoral duties, but they are not allowed to take Communion
9 Iran. When the Shah of Iran was forced into exile in 1979, Khomeini returned from exile in Paris to rule the country
10 Dennis
11 Richard Branson, founder of the Virgin 'empire'
12 Simon le Bon. He was rescued when his yacht *Drum* capsized during a race
13 a) *You*
14 Royal Ulster Constabulary – the police force of Northern Ireland
15 c) off Zeebrugge
16 Leading fashion designers
17 Neil Kinnock
18 Mick Jagger
19 Princess Margaret visited China in May, 1987 with her two children Viscount Linley and Lady Sarah Armstrong-Jones
20 Robert Runcie
21 Lady Diana Spencer
22 a) The Chancellor of the Exchequer
23 It is awarded for the best novel published in the year
24 Value Added Tax or VAT
25 The Royal Marines

27 · ST · Numbers and Measurements

1 A yard. In 1963 it was more accurately defined as 0.9144 metres
2 Eight. It was originally the length of a furrow in a ploughed common field
3 25.4
4 The metric system
5 One thousand
6 32° – the freezing point of water
7 The Famous Five (in the books by Enid Blyton)
8 One mile
9 366
10 The weight of precious stones, especially diamonds, and metals such as gold. One carat is equal to 0.25 grams
11 They both weigh exactly the same, one kilo
12 Minutes
13 29 days (and 12 hours, 46 minutes and 3 seconds)
14 Cubic centimetres
15 24. 'Four and twenty blackbirds, baked in a pie.'
16 Boeing aircraft
17 Sound
18 The Bible. It also has 1189 chapters, 31 173 verses and 774 746 words
19 Seven – pride, avarice, sloth, gluttony, lust, envy and wrath
20 Miles per hour
21 They are units for measuring pressure in meteorology
22 Calories. If you cut down on the number of calories in your diet, you will lose weight
23 Thirteen. The penalties for short-selling were so severe in the Middle Ages that bakers added an extra loaf (the vantage loaf) to every dozen they sold so they could not be accused of it
24 31
25 Three

28 · AC · Stage and Screen

1 J.R. Ewing in *Dallas*
2 Ballet companies. The Kirov is based in Leningrad and the Bolshoi is in Moscow
3 Clint Eastwood (in *Every Which Way But Loose* and *Any Which Way You Can*)
4 Andrew Lloyd Webber
5 The West End. Many of them are a few minutes' walk from Piccadilly Circus
6 Fozzie Bear
7 Mikhail Baryshnikov, who defected from USSR in 1974
8 Britain's National Youth Theatre. He took the appointment when he left the Royal Marines in 1987
9 Annie. The stage musical of that name was based on the American cartoon strip L'il Orphan Annie, and was later filmed
10 d) Michael Caine. Sean Connery and Roger Moore played James Bond in many movies. David Niven played him in *Casino Royale*
11 Chewbacca
12 Oscars. They are said to have got their name when a Hollywood secretary remarked that the statues reminded her of her Uncle Oscar. The actors in the photograph are John Travolta and Vanessa Redgrave
13 Adrian Mole (by Sue Townsend)
14 *Bugsie Malone*, the Alan Parker film that starred Jodie Foster
15 *Oliver Twist*. Lionel Bart wrote the musical on which the film was based
16 b) *Barnum*. Michael Crawford played the title role in the London production
17 Cinderella. It was written by Rossini
18 A diamond
19 *Star Trek*, the saga of the star ship *Enterprise* whose mission is to go where no man has gone before
20 *Desperately Seeking Susan*
21 *Fame*. The film was directed by Alan Parker
22 a) whistle. If you do you have to go outside and turn round three times
23 *Indiana Jones and the Temple of Doom*
24 Mary Poppins, based on the book by P.L. Travers
25 *The Mousetrap* by Agatha Christie. It opened in 1952 and is still on

29 · NW · Deserts, Jungles and Forests

1 Tarzan. The books were made into a series of successful films
2 No. They glide on flaps of skin found between their front legs and the sides of their bodies
3 Coniferous, which means evergreen
4 One
5 Yes. There are a few living in the Gir Forest in western India
6 a) Madagascar
7 Yes
8 Cacti
9 By rattling the bones in its tail
10 The eucalyptus tree
11 a) less than five inches a year
12 The Equator
13 Sherwood Forest
14 Nocturnal. Diurnal animals are active during the day
15 In its tail
16 c) around 2500
17 The lizard
18 On a pine tree
19 North of the equator, where there are greater land areas with cool climates
20 b) fat: it's a substance called albumin
21 The Canadian lynx
22 In nests in trees. It's a gorilla
23 Yes. On the rare occasions when it rains, flowers bloom briefly
24 Jungles
25 The jaguar. There are other large cats there, but the jaguar is the only one that belongs to the genus *Panthera*, the 'big cats'

30 · GH · Football

1 1966. They beat West Germany after extra time in the Wembley final
2 Greavsie – Jimmy Greaves
3 Kilmarnock, in Scotland
4 a) Edward II, in 1314
5 Notts County. It was founded in 1862
6 Glasgow Celtic. They beat Inter-Milan 2-1 in the 1967 final at Lisbon
7 Two. Brazil in 1958, 1962 and 1970, and Italy in 1934, 1938 and 1982
8 Bobby (the left picture) and Jack Charlton
9 a) 205 000 for the Brazil/Uruguay World Cup Final in Rio de Janeiro in 1950
10 Diego Maradona to give Argentina a 1–0 lead
11 White
12 45 minutes
13 b) 29. Bad weather caused the Falkirk v Inverness Thistle 1978–79 Scottish Cup tie to be postponed 29 times. Falkirk eventually won 4–0
14 Pelé. He was only seventeen when he played in his first World Cup final in 1958
15 Bobby Robson
16 Everton
17 *Today*
18 Rugby Football. It started at Rugby school in 1832 during a game of soccer when one of the boys picked up the ball and ran with it
19 Arsenal
20 Tottenham Hotspur. They play at White Hart Lane in north London
21 In 1930. Uruguay, the host nation, beat Argentina 4–2 in the final
22 Fédèration Internationale du Football Association. It's soccer's ruling authority
23 b) 24 feet (7.32 metres)
24 No
25 b) 15 lbs/sq. in

31 · PP · Europe

1 In Brussels, Belgium
2 Paris, France
3 West Germany. The 1972 Olympics were held in Munich
4 In the Netherlands. The Dutch have reclaimed millions of acres of land for cultivation
5 The Cotswolds in the west of England. It's the Thames
6 In the Swiss Alps. It's 14 685 (4477 metres) high
7 Spain
8 The Danube. It rises in the Black Forest in Germany and flows 2800 miles (4480 kilometres) until it reaches the Black Sea
9 East Germany. The city is the western part of Berlin, the capital of Germany until 1945
10 Four. France, Austria, Italy and West Germany
11 In the south of France
12 Greece and Turkey. It was entirely Greek until 1975 when Turkey invaded the island
13 The English Channel
14 The Vatican City – 108.7 acres (44 hectares)
15 German Democratic Republic (East Germany)
16 Spain. Pesetas are the currency there
17 33
18 The Channel Islands. Jersey and Guernsey are the largest islands in the group
19 In Athens, Greece. It's the Acropolis
20 Portugal – on the south coast of the country
21 Denmark
22 Sardinia
23 The Volga – 2292 miles (3688 kilometres) long
24 Liechtenstein
25 Spain. The Pyrenees are a range of mountains

32 · GT · Entertainment

1 Paul Daniels, the magician and quiz show host
2 A sound and light show. They often take place in famous buildings. Parts of them are lit up while a commentary tells the audience its history
3 Eric Morecambe
4 To attend the Royal Variety Show, when stars from all over the world perform for nothing and all the money raised is given to charity
5 By dancing. Terpsichore is the muse of dancing
6 Cilla Black, the hostess of *Surprise! Surprise!*
7 Selina Scott. She was also one of the first presenters of BBC's *Breakfast Time*
8 Roland Rat
9 A floor-show of dancing and singing, usually in a night club or restaurant
10 He is a mime artist
11 A puppet
12 Walt Disney. They were all full-length cartoons
13 Abraham Lincoln. He was shot by John Wilkes Booth on April 14, 1865
14 Dancing. They starred in many famous musicals
15 A mask
16 b) The Hollywood Musical
17 He was an escapologist who baffled audiences by getting out of padlocked boxes, handcuffs and strait-jackets
18 They are both hand puppets
19 Laurence. He was knighted in 1947 and made a life peer in 1970
20 She is a singer
21 The Archers
22 Conjurers. Prestidigitation means sleight of hand
23 b) an impressionist
24 By writing poems and songs. They flourished in France and northern Italy from the 11th to the 13th century
25 a) A piece of music. It became famous when it was used as the theme music for the film *The Sting* which was made many years after the tune was written

33 · ST · Transport

1 Concorde. It is used by British Airways and Air France
2 The QE2. It's the flagship of the Cunard Line
3 USS *Nautilus*. She was commissioned in 1955
4 The Duke of Bridgewater. He commissioned work to start on a canal in 1759 to carry coal from his mines at Worsley to Manchester
5 Sailing ships. The name comes from the Dutch word *kleeper*, which means fast horses
6 London. Work began in 1860 on an underground line from Paddington to the City of London
7 In New York
8 Black. Henry Ford said they could be any colour at all – as long as they were black
9 Germany. The D stands for Deutschland
10 Jaguar
11 The Owl and the Pussycat (in the poem by Edward Lear)
12 Barges
13 The M25
14 Sail it. It's a flat-bottomed Chinese boat
15 On a bobsleigh. The run is at St Moritz in Switzerland
16 They became the first men to fly a mechanically powered aircraft
17 Twice the speed of sound
18 They were airships. When the *Hindenburg* was destroyed in 1937 in a dreadful accident, the 'age of airships' came to an end
19 An Arab sailing vessel
20 Tram cars (trolley buses)
21 c) a man. It's a two-wheeled passenger cart
22 RMS *Britannia*
23 a) The Metro
24 The *Mayflower*, which sailed across the Atlantic in 1620
25 Air France

34 · AC · Word and Letters

1 Tom. The phrase Peeping Tom is now used to describe a nosy person
2 Boycott. When he was forced to collect increased rents by his employer, tenants refused to have anything to do with him
3 b) *Haute couture*
4 Master
5 DBE
6 His wife. It's Cockney rhyming slang
7 Sealed With A Loving Kiss
8 The Queen's. It means 'God and is my right'
9 L
10 Omega. It's the first letter in the illustration
11 'Le weekend'
12 The Prime Minister
13 The V-sign. He used it as a symbol of victory
14 M
15 *Repondez s'il vous plait* (Please reply)
16 Scrooge, the central character in *A Christmas Carol*
17 Queen's Counsel. QCs are barristers
18 Pounds (*librae*), Shillings (*solidi*) and Pence (*denarii*). Before Britain went decimal in 1971 there were 20 shillings in the pound, and twelve pennies in the shilling
19 The ancient language of India
20 Son of
21 Yawn
22 Railway companies. LMS was the London, Midland and Scottish Railway and LNER was the London and North Eastern Railway
23 A vowel. The others are A, E, I and U
24 BEA was British European Airways. BOAC was British Overseas Airways Corporation. BA is British Airways
25 It's the longest word in the English language without any vowels

35 · NW · Nature

1 South-west
2 Icebergs
3 The Gulf Stream. It flows across the Atlantic from the Gulf of Mexico
4 a) the study of weather
5 Slate
6 A flash of lightning
7 Revolves once
8 Chalk: that's why they are white
9 Water. Artesian Wells are found underground
10 They descend them
11 a) The Rockies
12 They grow down. Stalagmites grow up
13 It comes from trees. Amber is hardened (fossilized) resin
14 In the ocean. It's a coral reef that surrounds a lagoon
15 In the United States. It's in Arizona and it's the deepest canyon in the world
16 The Brazil nut
17 Desert
18 b) opal
19 They are all types of cloud
20 Yes. There are insects in every corner of the world
21 On high land. A plateau is an upstanding area of flat land usually surrounded by steep sides
22 An extinct volcano. (Although some volcanoes that were thought to be extinct have erupted!)
23 From trees
24 Green
25 To the top of Mount Everest, the highest point in the world

36 · GH · One to One

1 Karate
2 Fencing. They are all types of swords
3 Boris Becker in 1985
4 China
5 Two (unless you are playing doubles, in which case it's four)
6 Checkmate
7 Boxing
8 All-in wrestling
9 Heavyweight
10 Pakistani
11 32. There are 32 white ones as well
12 A fifteener. You add the score of the conker you smash to the number of conkers yours has previously smashed
13 Muhammad Ali: he said it when he was known as Cassius Clay
14 Roulette
15 Seven
16 Table tennis
17 c) Kathy Rinaldi beat Sue Rawlinson in a first round women's singles game in 1981 when she was 14
18 A snake's head
19 Nine
20 Six – yellow, brown, green, blue, pink and black
21 Spanish. It's Seve Ballesteros
22 Darts
23 A golfer
24 b) its spin
25 Your life!

37 · PP · Where in the World?

1 Rio de Janeiro, Brazil. It is well known for the huge statue of Christ on its summit
2 New York. Wall Street is a famous financial centre and Fifth Avenue is a fashionable shopping street
3 In the Vatican. They are the Pope's bodyguard
4 Sydney Harbour
5 In Venice
6 In Vienna, Austria, where many of the Strauss family lived and worked
7 On the top of Mount Everest, jumping one foot above the surface
8 In Moscow, in a mausoleum in the Kremlin
9 In Paris, in the caverns under the Opera House
10 The Atlantic. The West Indies are a chain of islands extending from the Florida Gulf to a few kilometres off the coast of Venezuela
11 In Egypt – the Pyramids are the only Wonders of the World still standing
12 At Windsor Castle in Berkshire
13 In Italy. They are the Italian equivalent of our motorways
14 b) Sao Paulo, with a population of over 10 000 000
15 Tanzania. Zanzibar is a large island separated from the rest of the country by a channel 22.5 miles (36 kilometres) wide
16 It is a kingdom. The present king, Baudouin, came to the throne in 1951
17 Djibouti, a tiny country on the tip of the Horn of Africa
18 Scotland and England. It was built by Emperor Hadrian (AD 76–138)
19 Egypt. It's where the Pyramids are
20 District of Columbia. The Americans wanted to discourage inter-state rivalry, so rather than have the capital in any of the states they created a separate district for it
21 In Agra, central India. It was built by the emperor Shah Jahan (1627–1658) in memory of his beloved wife. It took 22 years to build
22 In East Berlin, capital of East Germany
23 Denmark. Most of Greenland lies within the Arctic Circle
24 Paris. He was the son of King Priam of Troy who abducted Helen, thus starting the Trojan Wars. Paris, the city, is named after a tribe, the Parisii, who settled in France in pre-Roman times
25 Bangkok

38 · GT · Food and Drink

1 57
2 HP Sauce
3 Milk
4 They are all types of nuts
5 Coca Cola. It was created by John S. Pemberton
6 Caviar comes from the sturgeon. Any sturgeon caught in British waters must be offered to the Queen
7 Pancakes
8 The sheep
9 Tomato
10 Pizza
11 Vitamin C
12 Tea. The first two are Indian, the third is Chinese
13 Curds and whey
14 In China. They are all styles of Chinese cooking named after the areas where they originated
15 Baked Alaska, ice cream covered in meringue and baked in an oven
16 Scotland. Haggis is a mixture of oatmeal, offal and herbs, stuffed into the lining of sheep's stomach
17 The cacao plant
18 Caffeine
19 Hamburgers
20 Rice
21 An apple
22 Lemonade and beer
23 It's usually a herring, salted and smoked
24 b) Nellie Melba – a famous Australian opera singer
25 Cake

39 · ST · In Space

1. On the Moon. He was the first man to walk on it – in July 1969
2. Pluto. It was not discovered until 1930
3. Venus
4. The Milky Way. It is about 100 000 light years in diameter
5. *Sputnik I*. It was launched by the Russians in 1957
6. John F. Kennedy. He was assassinated in 1963
7. *The Sky At Night*. It's Patrick Moore
8. b) He was killed in a 'plane crash in 1968 while he was training for another space flight
9. Captain James Kirk, played by William Shatner
10. No. There have been other comets brighter than Halley's but it is the best known one
11. Pluto
12. b) the distance varies, but the average distance is 240 000 miles (384 000 kilometres)
13. Dr Who
14. It is the nearest star to the Earth (apart from the Sun). It's 4.3 light years
15. She was a dog, sent up in *Sputnik 2* on November 3, 1957
16. Krypton
17. They are constellations, or groups of stars. From the Earth we can see 88 of them
18. a) Edmund Halley (1656–1742), the British astronomer who predicted in 1705 that the comet would next appear in 1758 – which it did
19. The Moon passes between the Earth and the Sun
20. Russian. She was Valentina Tereshkova and orbited the Earth 48 times in *Vostok 6* in June, 1963
21. The Muppet Show
22. NASA – the US government agency responsible for space research
23. It exploded shortly after take off and all the astronauts in it were killed
24. The Great Bear
25. a) 2000, although many more are visible with a telescope

40 · AC · Myths and Legends

1. A dragon
2. The Phoenix
3. At Camelot. The picture shows the famous Round Table
4. Thor, the Scandinavian God of War
5. The robin; blood from the thorn spilled onto the bird's breast, and all robins have had red breasts ever since
6. Saint Andrew
7. Helen of Troy, wife of Menelaus, King of Sparta
8. According to superstition it is unlucky to look at the new moon through glass
9. The Catherine Wheel is named after Saint Catherine. According to legend when she was about to be executed by being tied to a wheel, her bonds miraculously snapped. But her luck did not hold: she was beheaded
10. An owl called Archimedes
11. Jupiter, the son of Saturn who he disposed
12. Jason, son of the King of Iolcus, and the Argonauts
13. Medusa. She was eventually slain by Perseus, son of Zeus
14. Because they believed that the song of the sirens would entice them on to the rocks
15. Twelve
16. His heel. His mother dipped him in the River Styx to make him invincible in battle, but because she held him by the heel, it remained vulnerable
17. Robin Hood
18. Forty, according to the old saying
19. Rip Van Winkle, in Washington Irving's *Sketch Book*
20. Inside a huge wooden horse
21. Sir Lancelot, as he rode to many-towered Camelot
22. Icarus, son of Daedalus. They made the wings to escape from Crete
23. The unicorn
24. Capulet
25. *El Dorado* – the kingdom of The Golden One

41 · NW · The Deep Blue Sea

1. 20 000 – in the book *20 000 Leagues Under the Sea*
2. A salmon. Salmon always return to the waters where they hatched to lay their own eggs
3. Popeye the Sailorman
4. The skeletons of dead sea creatures
5. The oyster. The largest ever found weighed 14 lbs (6.3 kg)
6. c) Neptune
7. Whales. The blue whale is the largest mammal in the world
8. The Irish Sea
9. The sturgeon, the fish that gives us caviar
10. The Pacific. It covers an area of 63 855 000 miles^2 (165 384 000 km^2)
11. An iceberg. The vessel was thought to be unsinkable but was holed and sank on her maiden voyage in 1912
12. A whale. Legend says that when Jonah was washed overboard he was swallowed by a whale and lived in its stomach for 40 days and nights
13. A great white shark
14. Live for long periods of time out of water
15. The Plimsoll Line. Named after Samuel Plimsoll, the MP who forced the law making the line essential on all British ships through Parliament
16. a) ice cream. Seaweed is an algae and when it is properly treated it can be used as an ingredient when making ice cream
17. Eight
18. Polaris submarines
19. A canoe, used mainly by Eskimos
20. Five, although some species have more
21. Captain Pugwash
22. He was *The Man From Atlantis*
23. A seascape
24. The Dead Sea in Israel/Jordan. It is the lowest spot on the Earth's surface
25. They are arms of the Southern (Antarctic) Ocean

42 · GH · Games

1. In China. It is a popular game throughout Asia
2. Croquet
3. He was playing bowls. It is said that he finished his game before heading for the flagship
4. Contract Bridge. They contract to make a certain number of tricks in the suit they bid in. Whoever makes the contract plays both his own and his partner's hand
5. Draughts
6. Triple letter. You add three times the value of the letter you place on it to your score
7. £200
8. Six
9. It is forbidden to talk. You have to relay a message to your team by miming it
10. The Bishop
11. Curling. When a stone is thrown, the curlers sweep the ice in front of it as it travels across the ice
12. They were game for a laugh in a show called *Game for a Laugh*
13. Six. They are whittled down to two finalists
14. The Olympic Games
15. Bingo. Legs Eleven is 11 and Key of the Door is either 18 or 21
16. Six. One in each corner and one half way down both of the longest sides. The player in the picture is Steve Davis
17. Highland Games. The caber is a heavy tree trunk
18. 180 – three treble 20s
19. Happy Families
20. b) Patience
21. He was playing bridge – and cheating
22. Dice! The correct singular of dice is die
23. Ring a Ring o' Roses
24. Grouse. The game shooting season starts on that date
25. a) Eton. It is a ball game played between two teams

43 · PP · The Past

1 Julius Caesar. In the Shakespeare play, Caesar's dying words are 'Et tu Brute' ('And you Brutus')
2 1914. The heir to the Austrian throne was assassinated in Bosnia. Austria, supported by Germany, declared war on Serbia; Russia came in on Serbia's side; Germany declared war on Russia and France, and marched through Belgium to attack; this brought Britain into the War and soon the whole world was at war
3 a) in 1936. Transmissions were stopped during the War
4 Egypt
5 Arrows. If your name is Fletcher, one of your ancestors was probably an arrow-maker
6 India
7 Christopher Colombus. At first he thought he had arrived in the Far East!
8 c) 240
9 The Great Fire of London, which started in a baker's shop in Pudding Lane and spread throughout the City
10 23. The last Pope John died in 1963
11 b) King Zog. He went into exile in Britain after his country was overrun by the Italians in 1939. He never returned
12 Napoleon Bonaparte (1769–1821)
13 He was French. His father was the Duke of Normandy
14 They were a dynasty of English kings, starting with Henry II in 1154 ending with Richard III in 1483
15 Her baby. It's a pram
16 Catherine of Aragon. Henry divorced her in 1533 to marry Anne Boleyn
17 Nicholas II. He and all his family were assassinated at Ekaterinburg in 1918
18 The Feudal System. They all worked for their Lord of the Manor
19 At Boston. American colonists boarded British ships and emptied their cargoes of tea into the water to protest that although they were taxed, they were not represented in Parliament
20 Martin Luther (1483–1546). He was a monk who was so against some of the policies of the Church that he protested against them. Hence, his followers were called 'Protestants'
21 The Royalists or Cavaliers, the supporters of Charles I
22 General Custer, in 1876
23 Mary II (1662–1694). She was the daughter of James II
24 The Duke of Wellington (1769–1852), victor of the Battle of Waterloo in 1815
25 The Hapsburg Austro-Hungarian Empire which was dissolved after the First World War

44 · GT · TV Time

1 a) Walford
2 On Sesame Street in the TV programme *Sesame Street*
3 Jimmy Savile O.B.E. His programme is *Jim'll Fix It*
4 Coronation Street. She's Hilda Ogden
5 On The Tum. There's a show called *Tickle On the Tum*
6 K9
7 Michael
8 Bobby Ewing in *Dallas*
9 Max Headroom
10 The Fonze in *Happy Days*
11 Los Angeles
12 Automan
13 Arthur Daly in *Minder*
14 *Good Morning Britain.*She also hosts *The Birthday Show*
15 Eamonn Andrews
16 Jon Pertwee
17 Les Dawson. He took over from Terry Wogan
18 *Hi De Hi.* She's Su Pollard
19 A helicopter
20 *Brookside*
21 Tom
22 *Connections*
23 *Blue Peter*
24 The Incredible Hulk
25 Super Bowl (American Football)

45 · ST · Eureka

1 Television. He first demonstrated it in 1926
2 RADAR. By sending sound waves into the air he could detect the presence of an aircraft 100 miles away
3 Alfred Nobel (1833–96)
4 a) Sir George Cayley's coachman. Sir George designed an early flying machine and sent his servant up in it in 1853. As soon as he landed, he resigned
5 The carpet sweeper
6 b) Clarence Birdseye. When he was in Alaska he noticed how the Eskimos stored fish in the ice to keep them fresh. When he went back to the States he started his frozen food company
7 Samuel Morse (1791–1872)
8 In a balloon. The one they 'launched' in November 1783 carried the first men to 'fly'
9 Archimedes. He was so excited when he realized that an object placed in water displaces its own mass of water, he ran naked down the street shouting 'Eureka' (I have found it)
10 Chinese. They were first flown there in the third century BC
11 The ball-point pen
12 Because they were working in New York and London
13 Potato Crisps. When a customer complained that his fried potatoes were much too thick, the cook deep-fried wafer thin slices of potato: the potato crisp was born
14 b) George Eastman in 1888
15 Worcestershire by two pharmacists Mr Lea and Mr Perrins
16 b) Drambuie. The family helped him escape from Scotland and as a reward he gave them the recipe for his own liqueur
17 He was a famous aircraft designer
18 The flushing toilet
19 Kirkpatrick Macmillan, a Scottish blacksmith in 1839
20 The Bunsen Burner
21 It fell on his head as he sat under an apple tree. This set him to wonder why things always fall downwards
22 Scissors
23 The submarine. His one-man craft the *Turtle* made the first submarine attack during the War Of American Independence. It was thwarted
24 The movable type printing press, in the 1450s. To be accurate, he re-invented it, for the Chinese had had the idea centuries before
25 The speed of light. He calculated that it travels at 187 371 mps (299 793 kms)

46 · AC · It's in the Book

1 Through a wardrobe
2 Little Grey Rabbit (by Alison Uttley)
3 Brown. The William books were written by Richmal Crompton
4 In a home for retired bears in Peru, in the Paddington books by Michael Bond
5 Pandora. (Adrian Mole's diary was written by Sue Townsend)
6 *Through the Looking Glass* (by Lewis Carroll)
7 Bigglesworth (by Captain W. E. Johns)
8 Mary Lennox in *The Secret Garden* by Frances Hodgson Burnett
9 Babar the Elephant, by Jan de Brunhoff
10 Winnie the Pooh and his friends (A. A. Milne)
11 They were both created by Ian Fleming
12 Thomas the Tank Engine (The Rev. W. Awdry)
13 Black Beauty (by Anna Sewell)
14 Captain Pugwash (John Ryan)
15 Nancy Drew (Carolyn Keene)
16 At Rugby School (Thomas Hughes)
17 A clock in J. M. Barrie's *Peter Pan*
18 Alice, in *Alice in Wonderland* by Lewis Carroll
19 Huckleberry Finn (in the books by Mark Twain)
20 Laura Ingalls Wilder
21 *The Old Man of Lochnagar*
22 Doctor Dolittle (by Hugh Lofting)
23 Father Christmas (by Raymond Briggs)
24 Beatrix Potter (1866–1943)
25 Toad (*Wind in the Willows* by Kenneth Grahame)

47 · NW · In the Garden

1 Roses
2 A herb garden
3 b) from bulbs
4 Dutch Elm Disease
5 a) Capability Brown (1716–83)
6 In Kensington Palace Gardens
7 In the Alps
8 The narcissus
9 A market gardener
10 Covent Garden. The fruit and vegetable market was moved to Nine Elms, in South London
11 Sweet peas
12 Potatoes
13 On the vine
14 In Japan. The flower is one of the emblems of Japan
15 Red
16 Apples
17 Because they eat garden pests and don't attack plants themselves
18 Yes
19 b) trimming bushes and hedges into artificial shapes
20 Yellow
21 Beans
22 Two years
23 The iris
24 b) 3.2 kg. One of that weight was grown by a Lincolnshire man in 1963. A Warwickshire man grew another the same weight in 1982
25 The fuchsia

48 · GH · All Sports

1 c) 18
2 Swimming
3 Yes
4 An archer. The word comes from two Greek words, *toxon* which means bow, and *philos* meaning loving
5 60 minutes. There are four quarters of fifteen munutes each
6 Green and white
7 Tennis. It is played for between US and British teams
8 On a horse. Competition dressage involves putting the horse through a sequence of movements
9 No. A forward pass is against the rules
10 A team of European golfers
11 b) the crawl
12 Six. Lords and The Oval ((in London), Old Trafford (in Manchester), Trent Bridge (Nottingham), Edgebaston (Birmingham) and Headingley (Leeds)
13 Cheltenham in Gloucestershire
14 Puck. Puck appears in *Midsummer Night's Dream* and the puck is the piece of vulcanized rubber which ice hockey players try to get into their opponent's goal
15 Baseball
16 Darts. Double top is double 20
17 An angler
18 You would be coming down – a rockface
19 The butterfly stroke
20 Fifteen. Two batsmen, two umpires, the bowler, the wicket-keeper and nine other fielders
21 Rugby League
22 White gloves
23 c) He was a famous baseball player
24 Water polo
25 You would be playing croquet

49 · PP · Exploration

1 Henry Morton Stanley (1841–1904) who came across Livingstone at Ujiji, in what is now Tanzania, in 1871
2 The Vikings, the Scandinavian race who are thought to have sailed as far as North America
3 Tutankhamun's in 1922. The picture shows Carter at work on Tutankhamun's sarcophagus
4 The Spanish conquerors who explored much of South and Central America
5 a) Abel Tasman. He discovered it in 1642–3 and called it Van Dieman's Land
6 He was Italian, but he sailed under the Spanish flag
7 The *Vittoria*, one of five ships that sailed from Spain in 1519 under the command of Ferdinand Magellan. The *Vittoria* was the only one to return
8 Huskies
9 Saint Christopher, who according to legend was a giant who one day carried a small child across a swollen brook
10 Yuri Gagarin. He orbitted the Earth in 1961 in *Vostok I*
11 *The Golden Hinde*. Drake was the first Englishman to circumnavigate the world
12 a) Scottish. He was born in Lanarkshire in 1813. He died in Africa in 1873 and his body was brought to Britain and buried in Westminster Abbey
13 Australia. He first sighted Botany Bay in 1770, explored the coast and named the area New South Wales
14 Sir Francis Drake's. She knighted him at an outdoor ceremony at Greenwich in 1967
15 Portugal. Henry (1394–1460) established a school for navigators and directed many voyages of discovery, but never went on one himself
16 *Swallows and Amazons*
17 b) Robert Falcon Scott (1868–1912). He and his team had hoped to be first to reach the South Pole but were beaten by Amundsen
18 John (c. 1450–c. 1498) and Sebastian (c. 1474–1557) Cabot
19 Newfoundland, in what is now Canada
20 None
21 a) Amerigo Vespucci (1451–1512) the Italian navigator, who made four voyages of discovery to the New World between 1497 and 1504
22 Sir Edmund Hillary (1919–)
23 a) the North Pole. He reached it on April 6, 1909
24 In the Antarctic in 1912
25 The Golden One

50 · GT · The Silver Screen

1 A young deer, in the Walt Disney film of the same name
2 Inspector Clouseau, the accident-prone detective
3 He bit an electric cable
4 Michael J. Fox in the film *Back to the Future*
5 Cinderella. Gemma Craven played her in the film
6 His nose grows
7 Truly Scrumptious
8 *The Empire Strikes Back*
9 Timothy Dalton who plays James Bond in *The Living Daylights*
10 She was a nanny
11 Darth Vadar
12 The Wizard of Oz. The film was called *The Wiz*
13 007
14 Gremlins
15 R2D2 and C3PO
16 Basil, the Mouse Detective
17 *Ghostbusters*. The picture shows the ghostbusting team
18 101. The film was *One Hundred and One Dalmatians*
19 Superman, played by Christopher Reeve
20 Sylvester Stallone
21 *Santa Claus – the Movie*
22 A lion
23 *The Muppet Movie*
24 'Sit!'
25 John

51 · ST · Facts and Feats

1 A calculator which is said to be the forerunner of the modern computer
2 The first sewing machine
3 Telecommunications satellites
4 a) textiles. Both were invented in the eighteenth century
5 Video recording machines
6 A motor scooter
7 a) he designed furniture during the eighteenth century
8 On a radio. MW is medium wave, LW is long wave and FM is frequency modulation
9 Leonardo da Vinci. He was born in Tuscany in 1452 and died in 1519
10 He was blind. His nickname was Blind Jack of Knaresborough. Despite his blindness, he fought at the Battle of Culloden in 1746
11 a) it crashed on its first outing and demolished a wall
12 It was the first oil well, sunk in the United States in the 1850s
13 Steam engines. *The Puffing Billy* was built in 1813 by William Hedley: *The Rocket* by George Stephenson in 1829
14 b) photography. Niepce (1765–1833) etched the first 'photograph' on pewter
15 It is the heaviest metal
16 The Egyptians
17 c) China
18 The microscope. Van Leeuwenhoek (1632–1723) was a Dutch cloth merchant who made magnifying glasses as a hobby
19 Four
20 They are made in Turin
21 The sound barrier, on October 14, 1947
22 b) China, before AD 1000
23 The pennyfarthing
24 It takes off vertically and does not need a long runway to land
25 It was made in 1797 by Andre Jacques Garnerin who jumped from a balloon at about 3280 feet (1000 metres) near Paris on October 22

52 · AC · Rhymes and Songs

1 Little Jack Horner
2 Wee Willie Winkie
3 Her holiday shoes
4 Three French hens
5 Pussy's in the well
6 There are three blind mice
7 He played a tune on his pipe and led all the children out of Hamelin. They were never seen again, apart from one lame boy who couldn't keep up
8 Silver
9 Widdicombe Fair
10 *Scarborough Fair*
11 A magic piano that could play by itself
12 The tiger in William Blake's poem, *Tiger! Tiger!*
13 Little Polly Flinders
14 Lavender's blue, Dilly-Dilly, Lavender's green
15 He was a miner who worked his claim during the gold rush of 1849
16 Daffodils, according to William Wordsworth's poem
17 My Bonnie lies over the ocean, My Bonnie lies over the sea
18 Three bags full
19 Robin, Kermit the Frog's nephew in *The Muppet Show*
20 Ten green bottles
21 She see-sawed
22 The man who wasn't there! (As I was going down the stair, I met a man who wasn't there. He wasn't there again today. I think he must have gone away)
23 In the Old Testament
24 10 000
25 The Three Blind Mice

53 · NW · Birds of a Feather

1 Sinbad the Sailor
2 True. Most male birds have better plumages than females
3 The bald-headed eagle
4 The goose that lays the golden eggs
5 The goldcrest, of the wren family
6 The chicken. There are more than 4 500 000 000 of them
7 A peahen
8 The cuckoo
9 The albatross. One was measured to have a wingspan of 11.9 feet (3.63 metres)
10 A brood or covey
11 The magpie
12 A gosling
13 A pen
14 The sparrow, with his arrow
15 No. They are too heavy for their small wings
16 Ravens
17 c) three years or more
18 Ducks
19 Golf. A birdie is one less than the course standard for a hole; an eagle is two less and the albatross three!
20 The lapwing
21 Because it was unable to fly to escape from hunters
22 Pigeons
23 An aviary
24 A woodpecker
25 Owls

54 · GH · Crafts and Hobbies

1 Stamps. The word comes from two Greek words, *philos* which means love of and *ateleia* which means stamps
2 Lace. Some complicated patterns involve working with hundreds of bobbins
3 Knot them. Macramé is a type of ornamental work made by knotting and weaving coarse thread
4 Stamp collecting. Sticky hinges are used to stick stamps into stamp albums
5 Knit and purl
6 An Evil Fighter
7 Lead. Birds, especially swans, can die from lead poisoning if they swallow lead tackle
8 It's horizontal. It is the spar to which a sail is fastened
9 Origami
10 Gardening. Potting on is putting a plant in a larger pot
11 An outdoor hobby. Contestants run over a course consisting of checkpoints which they find with a map and a compass
12 Falling through the air having jumped from a 'plane, before pulling the rip cord of your parachute
13 c) caves. Pot holers are speleologists
14 They are both fishermen. *Piscator* is the Latin word for angler
15 Twelve
16 A cat's cradle
17 Breeding tropical fish
18 a) numismatologists
19 Do It Yourself
20 Wood. Marquetry is in-laying one kind of wood in another
21 Bee-keeping. (From the Latin *apis* = bee)
22 Bird-watchers. Twitchers are very enthusiastic bird-watchers who go to great lengths to see a species they haven't seen before
23 Pots! They throw clay onto their wheels and fashion it into pots
24 A dog. Crufts is Britain's top dog show, held every year in London
25 a) butterflies and moths

55 · PP · Africa

1 Algiers
2 The Sahara. It extends 2800 miles (4480 kilometres) west to east and 940 miles (1504 kilometres) north to south
3 No. There are no tigers living wild in Africa. They are found only in Asia
4 a) 14 km – the narrowest point of the Straits of Gibraltar
5 South Africa. It means 'separate development', keeping the black and white races apart
6 b) it was the personal property of Leopold of the Belgians, but he administered it so badly that it was taken from him by the Belgian government
7 The Nile. It's 4160 miles (6695 kilometres) long
8 The Suez Canal. It was built by Ferdinand de Lesseps
9 Ethiopia
10 Kenya. Nairobi is the capital: shillings the unit of currency
11 France, until 1962 when it gained independence
12 Madagascar
13 The Atlantic Ocean
14 The Dark Continent
15 It lies north of the Equator
16 Safari
17 b) an African god
18 The ostrich
19 The Kalahari Desert in southern Africa
20 The sphinx. It is at Giza in Egypt and was built around 2550 BC
21 Zimbabwe, when it achieved independence in 1980
22 Zola Budd. She became British
23 The elephant
24 South Africa, mainly in Natal Province
25 Pygmies. They are nomadic hunters and gatherers who live in Tropical Africa

56 · GT · Animal Fun

1 He's the bear in *The Beano*
2 A handful of beans. When his mother threw them into the garden, they grew into the beanstalk
3 a) William Brown's in the William Books by Richmal Crompton
4 Brer Fox, in the Joel Chandler Harris stories
5 Rudyard Kipling (1865–1936)
6 A white rabbit
7 Rabbits, in the book by Richard Adams
8 The crocodile
9 Garfield, Jim Davis's cartoon-strip cat
10 A Collie (the one on the left of the picture)
11 He was a pig. After the farm animals took control of the farm, the pigs became the leaders and ended up treating the other animals as harshly as had the farmer
12 The Loch Ness Monster. It was first spotted as long ago as the thirteenth century
13 A bear
14 He is a tiger
15 The Cheshire Cat, in *Alice in Wonderland*
16 No. They eat fresh meat
17 Greyfriars Bobby. The picture shows a statue of him in Edinburgh
18 a) *The Eagle*
19 Nelson's Column, in Trafalgar Square. The lions were designed by Sir Edwin Landseer (1802–1873)
20 A lioness
21 Dick Turpin (c. 1706–1739) the famous highwayman
22 The fly
23 A dog. It was the star of several movies
24 The tortoise
25 A dog, called Nana

Photographic Acknowledgments
Australian Tourist Authority, Camerapix, Mary Evans
Picture Library, Johnstone Fact Finders, The Kobal
Collection, Monarchives, The MacQuitty International
Collection, New Zealand Tourist Board, Rex Features,
Sporting Pictures, Walt Disney Productions

Picture research by Debra Bradnum, Mary Corcoran,
Craig Dodd and Michael Johnstone

The publishers have made every effort to correctly
identify photographs, but will be pleased to correct
errors or omissions in future editions.

Cover acknowledgements:
Picture references for David Bowie and A-Ha courtesy of
London Features. Daley Thompson courtesy of Eamonn
McCabe. The *Star Wars* characters TM & © 1987
Lucasfilm Ltd. All rights reserved.
Spider-Man and the Incredible Hulk © 1987 Marvel
Entertainment Group, Inc. All Rights Reserved.

Questions for Trivial Pursuit by Michael Johnstone

Trivial Pursuit™